Highly effective Public Speaking Skills

80 modern skills to be an effective speaker

Dr. Y.Narasimha Raja
Ph.D., MBA, M.Sc. Psychology, M.Com, MTM
Assistant Professor – School of Management
Presidency University, Bengaluru
Email: ynr.phd@gmail.com; Web: www.ynraja.com
WhatsApp: +91-8073205840

The author articulated this book, with his research, various sources of books, electronic media, Social media, magazines, anecdotes, stories, journals, Interviewing with various experts, other speakers, and seminar participants. Primary and Secondary data have been considered. If any resemblance regarding the topic is purely coincidence as many examples and subject details have been collected from various sources. Regrettably, sources were not always renowned or available; hence, it became impractical to provide an accurate recognition.

MRP: Indian Rupees (INR) 300/-

ISBN: 9798887177502

Publishers: Notion Press

800, West El Camino Real #180,California USA 94040

Notion Press Media Pvt Ltd,

No.50, Chettiyar Agaram Main Road,Vanagaram,
Chennai, 600095, Contact +9144 46315631
Email : publish@notionpress.com
web: www.notionpress.com

Highly Effective Public Speaking Skills

Copyrights certificate
Awarded by the Government of India

Extracts from the Register of Copyrights

Dated : 27/05/2022

1.	Registration Number	:	**L-116094/2022**
2.	Name, address and nationality of the applicant	:	DR. YAGNAMURTHY NARASIMHA RAJA , 297, RAJA NIVAS, 11TH MAIN, 11TH CROSS, NARASIPURA LAYOUT,VIDYARANYAPURA, BANGALORE -560097-560097 INDIAN
3.	Nature of the applicant's interest in the copyright of the work	:	AUTHOR
4.	Class and description of the work	:	LITERARY/ DRAMATIC WORK HIGHLY EFFECTIVE PUBLIC SPEAKING SKILLS 80 MODERN SKILLS TO BE AN EFFECTIVE SPEAKER
5.	Title of the work	:	HIGHLY EFFECTIVE PUBLIC SPEAKING SKILLS
6.	Language of the work	:	ENGLISH
7.	Name, address and nationality of the author and if the author is deceased, date of his decease	:	DR. YAGNAMURTHY NARASIMHA RAJA , 297, RAJA NIVAS, 11TH MAIN, 11TH CROSS, NARASIPURA LAYOUT,VIDYARANYAPURA, BANGALORE -560097-560097 INDIAN
8.	Whether the work is published or unpublished	:	PUBLISHED
9.	Year and country of first publication and name, address and nationality of the publisher	:	2022 INDIA DR Y.NARASIMHA RAJA , 297, RAJA NIVAS, 11TH MAIN, 11TH CROSS, NARASIPURA LAYOUT, VIDYARANYAPURA, BANGALORE-560097 INDIAN
10.	Years and countries of subsequent publications, if any, and names, addresses and nationalities of the publishers	:	N.A.
11.	Names, addresses and nationalities of the owners of various rights comprising the copyright in the work and the extent of rights held by each, together with particulars of assignments and licences, if any	:	DR. YAGNAMURTHY NARASIMHA RAJA , 297, RAJA NIVAS, 11TH MAIN, 11TH CROSS, NARASIPURA LAYOUT,VIDYARANYAPURA, BANGALORE -560097-560097 INDIAN
12.	Names, addresses and nationalities of other persons, if any, authorised to assign or licence of rights comprising the copyright	:	YAGNAMURTHY JAYASIMHA SAKETH , 297, RAJA NIVAS, 11TH MAIN, 11TH CROSS, NARASIPURA LAYOUT, VIDYARANATAPURA, BANGALORE-560097 INDIAN YAGNAMURTHY NARASIMHA ABHAY , 297, RAJA NIVAS, 11TH MAIN, 11TH CROSS, NARASIPURA LAYOUT, VISYARANYAPURA, BANGALORE-560097 INDIAN
13.	If the work is an 'Artistic work', the location of the original work, including name, address and nationality of the person in possession of the work. (In the case of an architectural work, the year of completion of the work should also be shown)	:	N.A.
14.	If the work is an 'Artistic work' which is used or capable of being used in relation to any goods or services, the application should include a certification from the Registrar of Trade Marks in terms of the provision to Sub Section (i) of Section 45 of the Copyright Act, 1957	:	N.A.
15.	If the work is an 'Artistic work', whether it is registered under the Designs Act 2000 if yes give details	:	N.A.
16.	If the work is an 'Artistic work', capable of being registered as a design under the Designs Act 2000, whether it has been applied to an article through an industrial process and, if yes, the number of times it ...	:	N.A.
17.		:	HIGHLY EFFECTIVE PUBLIC SPEAKING SKILLS 80 MODERN SKILLS TO BE AN EFFECTIVE SPEAKER BOOK WRITTEN BY DR YAGNAMURTHY NARASIMHA RAJA IS UNIQUE AND ALL RIGHTS ARE RESERVED BY HIM.

	6565/2022-CO/L
D...	27/03/2022
Date of Receipt :	27/03/2022

Registrar of Copyrights

Dedication

This book is dedicated to
my beloved parents
Mr.Y.Subba Ramaiah & Mrs. Y.Rajeswari.

Never forget two people in life!

*The first person who was with you in every pain -**Mother** and*
*Second the person who lost everything just to make you win **-Father.***

Contents

Foreword

"Hearty Congratulations to you. Wishing you all the success! "

~Dr. Nissar Ahmed,Chairman,
Presidency Group of Institutions, Bengaluru.

"Public speaking is a great way of building personal development on many levels, since improving communication skills is helpful in almost every area of life. This book has the potential to greatly increase readers' confidence. Overcoming stage fear and public speaking jitters. public speaking abilities are a broad subject, the author has made every attempt to cover the topics and anticipates continuing the series."

~ Dr. D Subhakar -Vice Chancellor,
Presidency University, Bengaluru

Message content in "**Highly Effective - Public Speaking Skills**" and your awesome knowledge and experience spread across; '80 modern skills to be an effective speaker' is amazing fact.I am speechless on your concise and marvellous efforts puts on to build this booklet. My heartiest congratulations and best wishes to you and your aspirations.

~ Syed M Askari, Associate Director – A&F

Preface

"Everything is Easy, when you are Crazy,
but nothing is Easy, when you are Lazy "
–Swami Vivekananda

This quote has inspired the author to keep his maximum efforts to write this book.

In this book, 80 modern skills have been emphasized that can help you to be an efficient speaker.

It provides a broad range of information concisely and in an easy-to-read way. I assure, if these principles are applied in our practical life situation, we can defiantly view positive results within a fast span of time.

This book is written in simple English and self-explanatory for the purpose of readers' empowerment.

Never think I have nothing,
Never think I have everything,
but, always think
I have something & I can achieve anything

About Author

Dr. Y. Narasimha Raja is an International Trainer, Psychologist, Author, Coach, Mentor, Motivational speaker, counsellor and subject matter expert in his domain. He holds a Ph.D. degree in Management studies and multiple degrees that include Master of Business Administration, Master of Science in Psychology, Master of Commerce, and Master of Tourism Management.

He has more than 18 years of vast corporate experience in India & abroad. He has served various global corporate companies as Lead HR. He has a proven track of delivering responsibilities Professional merits

Professional Awards & certifications

- "Best HR Practitioner " certifications from Construction Industry Development Council (CIDC) during – Vishwakarma Awards for the year 2019 associated body of NITI Agog *(Formerly called Planning Commission of India).*
- National Prime Author Award -2021 by the Foxclues
- India Influence Award -2021 Best Corporate Trainer – Learning & Development – Organized By The The Crazy Tales fy 2021

- In his tenure, he has received several certifications for his performance from his organization viz *Merit of HR Operational Excellence, Well-done, systems & process, Great Job, Extra mile and many more.*
- He is certified as "Indian Management Styles" from the *Bangalore University* for the year 2002"

Personal Awards & Certifications

- 2002 Best Citizen Award - Andhra Pradesh Police
- 2000 Represented India South Asian Youth camp
- 1999 Represented India South Asian Youth Camp
- 2001 Pre Republic Parade – NSS
- 2002 N.C.C –Army Wing – C Certificate

Book Publications:

1. Highly Effective Parenting Skills
2. Highly Effective Teaching Skills
3. The best & smart Teaching techniques
4. Happy Parenting Skills
5. Stage Fear – 101 Techniques to overcome the stage fear.
6. Highly effective Public Speaking Skills

His lectures, articles, seminars have created a tremendous impact on people and shown them the path to achieve success. Apart from his corporate experience, currently, he is serving as an Assistant professor at Presidency University, Bangalore.

Readers note

The author has kept his highest efforts in writing this book. He respects all the readers and their feelings. He believes that all the readers are positive attitude icons. This book is written in simple English a self-explanatory mode for the purpose of reareader'spowerment.

He sees, the readers to be Swan bird,
Who can separate milk from a mixture of water?

If you find any errors in this book, kindly forgive and observe the goodness of this book.

Let us be a player in life, who runs for the goal & not a referee who looks for the faults

Language is just a means of communication; author has seen many thought provoking incidents, which has made him to pen down this book to spread awareness among us. Please extend positive thoughts &awareness of this book in the society.

With you and for you

Dr.Y.Narasimha Raja
Ph.D., MBA, M.Sc. Psychology, M.Com, MTM
Email: ynr.phd@gmail.com; Web : www.ynraja.com

Learning sessions with the Author

My sincere thanks goes to all the readers and their family members. Having trust on me and this subject book.

I guarantee this book will drive help to bring trust & happiness in family. Reading the book is not enough and it should come in practicality.

I am selling this book for a nominal cost, my primary intention is not to earn monetary profit from this book instead I believe in benefitting the reader out of this book.

As a value addition to the readers, I will be imparting learning sessions by modes of videos, email, and Whatsapp with the readers. To avail of these services, readers are requested to get connect with the author.

For Training, consultation, seminars get connect

Dr.Y.Narasimha Raja

Ph.D., MBA, M.Sc. Psychology, M.Com, MTM

Email: ynr.phd@gmail.com; Web : www.ynraja.com

WhatsApp: +91- 8073205840

Chapter-1

What is Public Speaking?

*"A wise man speaks because he has something to say,
A fool speaks because he has to say something."-Plato*

There is no shortcut to an Impart the great speech. Public speaking is not having simple talk or reading the speech in front of an audience. "Public speaking is a systematic process, an act and an art of making a speech before an audience". The appropriate use of public speaking effectively is actually tougher than anticipated, mostly in front of an audience.

"Grasp the subject, the words will follow."-Cato

Effective public speaking will improve through practice and hard work. Public speaking is a unique skill. To learn public speaking skills, age has no limit, education is not a boundary, gender is not important,

your qualification may not require, there is no differentiation between rich and poor to inculcate these skills and practices. Public speaking is the most important skill to have in all phases of life. Public speaking is applicable to all occupations, professions, and vocations. There is a myth that few people think that it will be applicable and restricted to only business professionals.

Public speaking is an exexpert skill that will apply and transform our every day. It opens nopensays to improve ourselves. It permits you to inhale new life into your thoughts and spread them to a more extensive audience. If your Idea is transformed to the audience, now it belongs to the individuals who can do the knowledge transformation to other people, in this way sharing the knowledge, ideas, and thoughts further.

The specialty of public speaking will be addressing multiple audiences speaking before whole countries, or any place andon any topic. Public speaking can mean persuading, convincing, an influencing others.

- Public speaking / a presentation that is given live before a multitude of people.
- Public speeches can cover a various range of themes or topics.
- The objective of the speech might be to teach, engage, or affect the audience members.

- Public speaking with preparation. There might be a chance for interaction or might not be an interaction between the speaker and audience.
- Public speaking also known as oratory is given speech/conversation on a face-to-face personal live audience (formally and informally) between a group of people and the speaker.

It might be in Business, student presentations, political campaigns, or entertainment events. The extent of scope for public speaking is interminable i.e. endless. Public speaking includes a thought process, regardless of whether it be to be inspired, entertain, persuade, inform public speaking includes preparation and speaker involvement in the subject as well as speaker should overcome from the stage fear, tension, anxiety, or nervousness to impeach great speech. In the event that the speaker is having less insight-experienced speakers, public speaking includes conquering tension to adequately convey a speech.

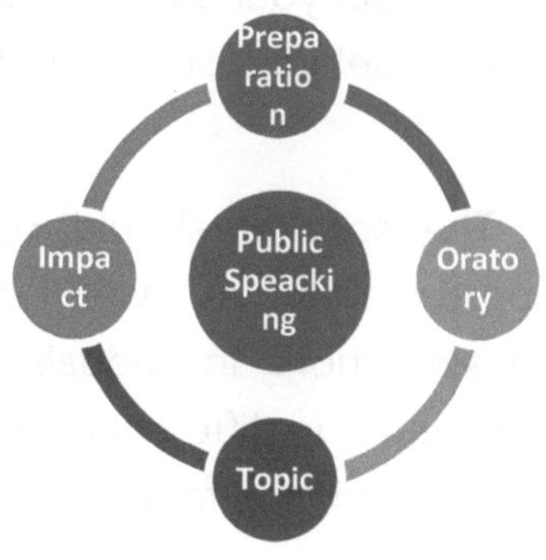

The enchantment of public speaking lies in

1. Speaker
2. Communication
3. Idea
4. Audience

During the presentation/speech, a speaker's idea should match the expectations of the audience. In the event that the subject/topic is not relevant to their lives, the audience will quickly lose interest.

The effective public speaker will practice following the steps

1. Source your subject
2. Get into your subject
3. Get your subject into yourself
4. Get your subject to know about your audience.

The speaker should connect with the audience appropriately as well ideas by directing their consideration. Individuals who perform with great confidence in different domains of life will probably see that confidence falter when it comes to the speaking public.

Swami Vivekananda 1893Chicago speech photos

Chapter-2

Importance of Public Speaking

"There are always three speeches, for every one you actually gave. The one you practiced, the one you gave, and the one you wish you gave." - Dale Carnegie

Public speaking is the most important skill to have in all phases of life. Public speaking is applicable to all occupations, professions, and vocations. There is a myth that few people thinks that it will be applicable and restricted to only business professionals.

Public speaking skills empower other inherent skills of individuals. Personal emotions may create temporary fear once you overcome these fears confidently will lead the success.History is the determined people who tackled their most impressive blessing have formed an evidence set of experiences: their voices.

Public speaking is an expert that will apply and transform our everyday. The ways to improve ourselves. It permits you to inhale new life into your thoughts and spread them to a more extensive audience. Once your thought and Idea is transformed to an audience, now it belongs to the individuals who can do the knowledge transformation to other people, in this way sharing the knowledge, ideas, and thoughts further.

The voices of energetic people are answerable for making the world that we live in today. Their thoughts alone would not have made these changes; however, there is no blockage that can stop your effective public speaking skills.

Be guaranteed that public speaking proceeds in many forms every day across the globe. Do you project yourself as an effective public speaker? And if you do, as a speaker do you realize yourself as prepared, confident, ready, and effective? Alternatively, do you see as who is stressed, unsure, nervous, of what to impart the speech or presentation, and being stressed as they are going to sense they are going to fail to communicate their message to the audience? Let us discuss with a small moral story that explains the importance of Public speaking in our personal and professional life.

Some time ago, there were two woodcutters named Peter and John. They were frequently in constant competition over who cut more trees. Therefore, one day, they chose to hold a competition to decide the winner. The principles were basic—whoever produces the most wood in a day wins.

Therefore, the following day morning, the two of them took up their situations in the woods and began cleaving away in their quickest conceivable speed. This went on for an hour before Peter out of nowhere halted. At the point when John understood that there was no hacking sound from his adversary's side, he thought: "Ah Ha! He should be worn out as of now!" In addition, he kept on chopping down his trees with twofold the speed. A fourth of an hour passed, and John heard his rival cleaving once more. So the two of them continued simultaneously. John was beginning to feel fatigued when the slashing from Peter halted indeed. Feeling aroused and smelling triumph nearby, John progressed forward, cheerfully.

This went on a general day. Consistently, Peter would quit cleaving for fifteen minutes while John continued going determinedly. Therefore, when the opposition finished, John was very certain that he would take the victory. In any case, to John's bewilderment, Peter had really chopped down more wood. How did this at any point occur? "How is it possible that you would have slashed down a bigger number of trees than me? I heard you quit working each hour for fifteen minutes!" shouted John. Peter answered, "Indeed, it's truly basic. Each time I halted work, while you were all the while slashing down trees, I was sharpening my hatchet."

The moral of the story is to have an effective tool to progress in your life, I can say confidently, "Highly effective public speaking skills" is the sharpen axe to progress in your personal and professional life.

Public speaking is an extraordinary method of building self-awareness on numerous levels, since improving communication skills is useful in every everyday issue. What is seen consistently, however, is that the increased confidence level has created from dominating the specialty of public speaking will pour out over into different everyday issues.

Chapter No.3

Benefits of Public Speaking

"You can speak well if your tongue can deliver the message of your heart" - John Ford

How public speaking can advance individual life, proficient life, and the rest of the world. Public speaking is an incredible confidence promoter. Accomplishment in public speaking demonstrates inventiveness, decisive reasoning abilities, administration capacities, balance, and polished methodology characteristics, which are truly significant for the work market. Public speaking is an extraordinary way to display your knowledge, skills, talents abilities, and capacities. For experts who need to construct an individual brand, increment publicity, or procure a standing as a specialist, public speaking is an incredible method for encouraging those aspirations.

Professional success

Highly effective public speaking skills can assist with professional success as they show creativity, imagination, basic reasoning skills, critical thinking, administration capacities, balance, and characteristics that are entirely important for the work market. Public speaking will help you get a new job and career progression in your profession. Employers will often pick the person who records "Public Speaking" as an exceptional skill and competency.

Qualities	Rating (on a 5-point scale)
Communication skills	4.7
Strong work ethic	4.6
Initiative	4.5
Interpersonal skills	4.5
Motivation/Initiative	4.5
Problem-solving skills	4.5
Teamwork skills	4.5
Analytical skills	4.4
Flexibility/Adaptability	4.3
Computer skills	4.2
Detail-oriented	4.1
Leadership skills	4.1
Technical skills	4.1
Organizational skills	4
Self-confidence	3.9
Tactfulness	3.8
Friendly/Outgoing personality	3.7
Creativity	3.6
Strategic planning skills	3.3
Entrepreneurial skills/Risk-taker	3.2
Sense of humour	3

According to jobweb.com, employers rate the importance of candidate skills/qualities (November 2009, p. 23). Job Outlook 2010 NACE Research. The national Association of Colleges & Employers.

1. **Improve communication skills**At the point when you compose a speech, you need to consider the best system, procedure, & expression to convey your message to the crowd. This sort of reasoning can assist you with improving your communication skills in different parts of your life.

2. **Self-improvement**Communication skills are essential for individual and expert achievement. Setting up speech powers speakers to make a stride back and contemplate successful approaches to impart.

3. **Make a professional connection**Public speaking commitments are acceptable spots to meet others who share your inclinations. You will see that individuals approach you after your introduction to participate in the discussion. It makes it a lot simpler to make new social associations. Make new social associations with public speaking.

4. **Grow your expert organization** Another advantage of public speaking is that when you talk at an occasion, you will abruptly find that everybody needs to converse with you. This is a significant chance for making companions, building business contacts, and producing business.

Chapter –4

Five Principles of Public Speaking Skills

"Knowledge speaks, but wisdom listens."
-Jimi Hendrix

The Romans, as well as the Greeks, were much contributed of Public speaking skills. One amongst such citizensTullis Cicero – by profession a lawyer, philosopher & politician who gained prominence as Rome's best orator. Around 50 B.C. Cicero wrote "De Oratore" in this he has explained which "Five Canons of Rhetoric" that the process of public speaking preparation consists of five main steps:

1. Invention
2. Arrangement
3. Style
4. Memory
5. Delivery

1. Invention (Inventio):

Invention is the systematic process of developing and refining your speech. As per Mr.Aristotle demonstration, invention must considered needs, interests, Audience background Stasis.

Stasis is a procedure designed to help a rhetorician develop and clarify the main points of his argument.

2. **Dispositio (arrangement):**

   The process of arranging and organizing speech for maximum impact.

3. **Elocutio (style):**

   The process of determining how you present your arguments using figures of speech and other rhetorical techniques.

4. **Memoria (memory):**

   The process of learning and memorizing your speech so you can deliver it without the use of notes. Memory-work not only consisted of memorizing the words of a specific speech, but also storing up famous quotes, literary references, and other facts that could be used in impromptu speeches.

5. **Actio (delivery):**

   The process of practicing how you deliver your speech using gestures, pronunciation, and tone of voice.

Chapter –5

Modern skills to be efficient speaker

"They may forget what you said, but they will never forget how you make them feel" -Carl W Buechner

Public speaking will enable our life through a

phenomenal wellspring of advantages. Public speaking will open the path of advantages to impact and influence others. Public speaking will help us to take incredible steps in our personal and professional life. The capacity to empower, motivate, illuminate, engage, or convince through public speaking is what the great traits of top management are to workers. All successful leaders and personalities have utilized public speaking to achieve their vision, mission, objectives that can be carried forward by the followers. The high impact of public speaking will affect your prosperity, success, profit and happiness.

If you are an active participant and a key contributor to a team, you will become the facto leader. In this case, the speaker willingly and voluntarily imparts the presentation or speech very comfortably, confidently in front of the audience. In this phase as a speaker, you accept this presentation is an opportunity, not a difficulty.

Employers seek employees with a talent for public speaking. Superiors favour subordinates who have a proven record of accomplishment of exhibiting the talent of communication and ability to speak publicly. The world looks for leaders who can inspire people with the power of their words.The confidence that comes from the ability to speak publicly implants itself into all other aspects of life. Public speaking is significant; it is a unique skill that will ever take you closer to achieving your ambitions.

Most individuals have a stage fear of speaking in public. Despite the fact that you might be thinking that speaking will not be essential in your life, actually, people involved in their profession, engaged in various functions, they will be shocked at the number of opportunities that we should give speeches. These changes can develop individual professional, personal skills, impact society, and advance your progression.

Skill No.1

Recognize who you are? In addition, what your strengths are.

"With the right mind-set, you can turn your weakness into your strengths"

Knowing self and strengths is nothing but identifying your talents. The talent of the speaker will take until the role but knowing self & strengths will lead to further progress.

- ✓ Knowing self, the speaker will be happier and the speech will be more impactful
- ✓ Less inner conflict
- ✓ Speaker will have great self-control
- ✓ Speaker will opt for the correct decision making
- ✓ Allows you to grow even more
- ✓ Realizing your qualities help increment your mindfulness.
- ✓ Uplift the productivity
- ✓ Builds commitment and maintenance.

Skill No.2

Have self confidence

Every man who has become great owes his achievement to incessant toil ~ Sir M. Visvesvaraya

Confidence permits public speakers to talk with clarity. Confidence is a critical part of being successful in any circumstance. One of the segments where confidence truly matters is public speaking.

- ✓ Public speaking deals with communicating your message to the audience. Confidence in public speaking is significant.
- ✓ Confidence will transform the public speaker from negative thoughts to positive thoughts.
- ✓ A confident speaker will overcome self-doubt.
- ✓ More peace of mind and less stress
- ✓ Allows the speaker to fulfil the goals
- ✓ The speaker will be a positive motivator.
- ✓ Confidence improves the bonding between the speaker & the audience.
- ✓ Gives leadership trait to deliver your speech
- ✓ Increased sense of self-worth
- ✓ Less fear and anxiety
- ✓ Feeling valued.

Skill No.3

Learn about various kinds of public speaking and how to deliver a better speech.

"If you can speak, you can influence. If you can influence, you can change lives"

Public speaking is the point at which you remain in front of a crowd of people and convey a discourse on a topic. This could be at a formal or an informal event. As public speaking has become a genuine profession, trained abilities, and procedures to talk well. To be a decent speaker, you should know the four kinds of public speaking and the eccentricities of every one of them.

1. Speaking to Inform
2. Speaking to Persuade
3. Speaking to Motivate
4. Speaking to Entertain

Speaking to Inform

At the point when you impart the speech before a group of people to exchange information on a specific

topic or issue, it is supposed to be an informative discourse. Corporate presentations, workshops in universities, seminars, class introductions in schools are a few instances of informative talks.

The speech should be short. The accomplishment of an informative speech will depend on how much the audience has understood the speech. It depends on the accuracy in the subject, the exactness of your message. Individuals should have the option of trusting the information that they are getting from you is correct.

Speaking to Persuade:

Persuasive speaking will in general be the most impressive. Politicians, sales and marketing professionals, lawyers and this kind of professionals will persuasive speaking. This kind of speaking requires continuous practice on voice modulation and command over the language that will influence/impact persuade the audience. The persuasive speaker has a stake in the result of the speech. Persuasive speeches are systematic speeches where you attempt to change the audience's views. These speeches mean to impact and change their perspectives on one or the other subject matter expertise. High enthusiasm is required to impart these kinds of speeches.

Speaking to Motivate:

Motivational speeches are exceptionally passionate, emotional, and applicable to all situations. Speakers try to stir, encourage, inspire, energize and animate an audience to apply in their personal and professional life.

Corporate Trainers, motivational speakers apply these skills to improve the productivity of the employees in an organization. The aim is to motivate and inspire enough people to take specific actions, tasks and results. This is a powerful level of speaking. Very few effective speakers have achieved this level of expertise in the art of persuasion where they could so deeply convince people to move into action.

Speaking to an audience is a more significant level of persuasive speaking. Here, the speaker goes to the stage past influence and persuading. The point is to spur enough individuals to find a particular way—to act. This is an incredible degree of speaking. Not very many individuals have accomplished this degree of authority of the craft of influence where they could so profoundly persuade individuals to move right into it.

Speaking to Entertain

Ceremonial speeches are one more type of public speaking generally given a College, schools, birthday parties, farewell (retirement) parties at corporates, weddings, and so on. The influence of personal emotions is very high in this speaking to entertain.

The speech can be happy, entertaining, or passionate, with humour to suit the event. You should take care not to hurt anyone's feelings. Keep in mind, your audience is assembled to make some great memories. Try not to demolish the decorum.

Entertaining speeches will be speeches intended to enrapture an audience's consideration and amuse or interest them while conveying a reasonable message. Speakers participate in entertaining speeches mostly at extraordinary events (e.g., weddings, burial services) or are approached to convey a feature address.

Skill No.4

Understand the similarities between Public Speaking & Conversation

"Effective communication is 20% what you know and 80% how you feel about what you know." -Jim Rohn

How much time do you go through every day conversing with others? In the normal time, approx. 30% of her or his waking hours are spent in discussion. Please utilize a wide scope of abilities when conversing with individuals. These abilities incorporate the accompanying:

- ✓ Both public speaking and conversation have similarities in terms of time for the interaction and message.
- ✓ Public speaking and conversations have an equal system of communication to the other person.
- ✓ Both public speaking and everyday conversation must have an impact on the life of the listeners.
- ✓ Both public speaking and conversation have similarities in terms of communication channels and directions.

Skill No.5

Understand the distinctions between Public Speaking & Conversation

"There is only one rule for being a good talker – learn to listen." ~ Christopher Morley

In spite of their similarities, public speaking and regular discussion are most certainly not indistinguishable. Imagine that you are recounting a story to a companion. At that point, envision yourself recounting the story to a gathering of seven or eight companions. Public speaking is the process of speaking to an audience in a structured, intentional way proposed to educate, impact, or engage the audience members.

The conversation is a type of spontaneous communication, an unconstrained correspondence between at least two people of etiquette. There are differences that put public speaking aside from discussion: hierarchical construction, utilization of formalized language, and technique for conveyance.

Speeches include thoughts, organized & organized processes. Speeches are often conveyed in purposeful, deliberate settings and settings, while discussions may emerge suddenly. Conversation can jump up anywhere. Public speaking is often coordinated into occasions and scenes with a set time and area. Public speeches may. Likewise, fall inside certain time requirements, though discussions can be as brief or as long as those included will take part.

The simple difference between Public Speaking & conversation

Public Speaking	Conversation
Formal (dress, posture, gestures, distractions, language)	Informal
Requirement or Necessity	Entertainment
Pre planning & practice	Spontaneous
Structured (time limits, uninterrupted)	Unstructured
Delegated roles	Shared Roles
Changing Environment	Stable Environment
Responsible	Forgiving
Tuned to audience	Equal
Spontaneity	Spontaneous
Colourful	Muted
Compelling	Comfortable

- Public speech is well organized than casuals
- Professional / Formal language utilization
- Method of delivery

Skill No.6

Organize the framework of your speech

Speak in such a way that others love to listen to you. Listen in such a way that others love to speak to you

IBC Principle: Public speaking is an exceptionally organized structure than normal conversations. Speeches and public speaking are much structured organized in daily conversation. A public speaker puts together their considerations in a speech by utilizing three essential underlying components

- **Introduction**
- **Body**
- **Conclusion**

Speeches are intentionally structured and coordinated, though discussions are definitely not.

1. Introduction of Speech

"Begin at the beginning" While this may be a line from the fantastical universe of Lewis Carroll's Alice in Wonderland, it is a great recommendation when contemplating the introduction to your speech. The introduction is the initial segment of your speech that will establish the vibe tone for all your speech.

An introduction can make or break a speech

With the introduction, you have the ability to capture your audience's special attention and interest while at the same time giving them a comprehension of what they're going to hear for the following five, ten, or even an hour.

Express Your Purpose

Catch Your Audience's Attention. Your introduction is not just an introduction about what you plan to speak, but also an introduction of who you are and why you are the appropriate individual to speak about your subject

Layout your Agenda

It is useful for the audience to think concerning what you intend to talk about. Utilize your introduction as a chance to impart your speech to the audience.

Composing Your Introduction

As strange as this might appear, you really need to compose your introduction last. Since the introduction is regularly utilized as a blueprint for the central issues of your speech, it is useful to have composed the whole speech to have the option to distil your speech into its significant focuses and contentions. When you have your whole speech composed less your introduction, it is a lot simpler to see just which focuses arise as your significant focuses.

2. Body of the Speech

The body of your speech is where the Public Speaker carefully describes every one of your central matters. The body is the place where you recount your story.

- Build up. Your Purpose
- Normally, there are three general reasons why you may be giving a speech:
- To engage, to illuminate, or to contend a point.
- Decide your Main Points
- Choose How you Will Tell your Story
- Articulate the Body

3. Conclusion of the speech

Utilize your conclusion as a great opportunity, to sum up the main points of your speech.

- Try not to repeat the main points, as it is word-to-word.
- Consider finishing your speech with an extra account or citation that catches the topic of your speech.
- Try not to present any new points or steady proof/evidence into your conclusion, as it will confuse the audience.

Skill No.7

Use of Language in an Appropriate Manner

Our language is the reflection of ourselves. A language is an exact reflection of the character and growth of its Speakers - Cesar Chavez

Public speaking requires more professional and formal language to be conventional to the audience. Slang, language, bad grammar, jargon, and have little place in public speeches. When you will be having a conversation with your dearest companion or friends either face to face, message or talk, you may find that your language and tone are casual.

Public speaking formalizes language significantly more. At the point when speeches are intended to "advice, influence, or engage," they require a specific custom of speaking contrasted with an easy-going discussion between companions. Slang, profanity, and helpless grammar may be acknowledged between companions yet are certainly not proper for any sort of public location or speech.

"The art of communication is the language of leadership" by James Humes.

Skill No.8

Practice PREP framework

Our goals can only be reached through the vehicle of a plan. There is no other route to success.~Picasso

By practicing the PREP formula, you can be a successful Public speaker. The PREP framework is a simple, viable, and effective approach to giving a speech. In the event that you have at any point been called up to impart the speech within the short notification, the PREP framework will help to get fruitful results.

Full form of PREP is

1. **Point**
2. **Reason**
3. **Example**
4. **Point**

1. Point (CLAIM):

The claim deals with what you think. Express your case. Start by expressing your primary point, claim, or suggestion. In a short speech, it is ideal to zero in on only one point with the goal that you do not lose your audience. In a more extended speech, utilize a progression of PREPs to make various focuses and support them.

2. Reasons:

The reason deals with why you feel and think that. Offer motivations to clarify why your point is valid. Back up or support your case with proof from research, reality, facts & figures, information, data, statistics.

3. Proof or Example (s):

It explains how you know, realize that to be true. Give more examples, case studies. Give at least one model/outlines to help your primary concern (case) and the reasons given previously.

4. Point:

Conclude by showing how your position is correct (logically, scientifically, scripturally, biblically, practicality for all intents and purposes, and so forth) this assists your audience in recollecting that it.

Skill No.9

Monroe's Motivated Sequence

All the great speakers were bad speakers at first - Ralph Waldo Emerson

Monroe's Motivated Sequence (MMS) is an organizational pattern used to develop a sense of want or need in the audience, satisfy that want or need, and help the audience be enthusiastic about the advantages of that solution. Monroe's Motivated Sequence is a five-step progressive method of persuasion, developed by Alan Monroe in the mid-1930s. This method is used to encourage people to take action and prime your audience to make an immediate change. Monroe's Motivated Sequence is seen in many real-life situations.

Monroe's motivated sequence emphasizes the action the audience can take. He has taken the audience from the situation that is hopeless to the active mode. It also helps the audience feel like the speaker knows the problem at hand and is listening to them instead of just tuning them out. It emphasizes that the audience can do.

1. Attention
2. Need
3. Satisfaction
4. Visualization
5. Action

MONROE'S MOTIVATED SEQUENCE- THE FIVE STEPS

STEP	FUNCTION	IDEAL AUDIENCE RESPONSE
Attention	to get the audience to listen	"I want to hear what you have to say"
Need	to the get audience to feel a need or want	"I agree. I have that need/want
Satisfaction	to tell audience how to fill need or want	"I see your solution will work"
Visualization	to get audience to see benefits of solution	"This is a great idea"
Action	to get audience to take action	"I want it"

Monroe's Motivated Sequence Checklist

Step in the Sequence	Yes	No
Attention Step		
Gained audience's attention	[ ]	[ ]
Introduced the topic clearly	[ ]	[ ]
Showed the important topic to the audience	[ ]	[ ]
Need Step		
Need is summarized in a clear statement	[ ]	[ ]
Need is adequately illustrated	[ ]	[ ]
Need has clear ramifications	[ ]	[ ]
Need clearly points the audience	[ ]	[ ]
Satisfaction Step		
Plan is clearly stated	[ ]	[ ]
Plan is plainly explained	[ ]	[ ]
Plan & solution are theoretically demonstrated	[ ]	[ ]
Plan has clear reference to practical experience	[ ]	[ ]
Plan can meet possible objections	[ ]	[ ]
Visualization Step		
Practicality of plan shown	[ ]	[ ]
Benefits of plan are tangible	[ ]	[ ]
Benefits of plan relate to the audience	[ ]	[ ]
Specific type of visualization chosen (positive method, negative method, method of contrast)	[ ]	[ ]
Action Step		
Call of specific action by the audience	[ ]	[ ]
Action is realistic for the audience	[ ]	[ ]
Concluding device is vivid	[ ]	[ ]

Skill No.10

Attention

One of the greatest gifts you can give to anyone is the gift of attention. ~Jim Rohn

Attention is the first step that the audience will focus. Through the attention-getting devices, Public speakers aim to do two basic things:

1. Get the audience's attention.
2. Get the audience into the topic.

1. Get the audience's attention:

The most precious gift you can give someone is the gift of your time and attention. It is part of attention. Get the attention of your audience. Use telling stories, humor, a shocking statistic, fact, quote, engaging question, or a rhetorical question – anything that will get the audience to sit up and take notice.

2. Get the audience into the topic:

- Relevance the audience,
- Humorous conversation with story
- Emphasize the importance of the topic
- Focus a startling statement
- Posing a question (maybe rhetorical)
- Curiosity or suspense

Skill No.11

Create a Need of your speech

To be happy in life, you must learn the difference between what you want vs. Need

The topic is applied to the psychological needs of the audience members. In this step, you will work to get your audience to feel a need or want, whichever you determine to be appropriate. This is accomplished via four steps:

Statement: The Statement gives a definite, concise declaration of what the need or want is.

Illustration: It gives one or more examples illustrating the need or want. This is where you try to "paint pictures" verbally to really get the audience to feel that need or want.

Ramification: Ramification here speaker can offer additional evidence, such as statistics/testimony/examples which give even more weight to the need or want.

Pointing: It deals where you really point out how this need or want is directly related and important to the audience.

Skill No.12

Justify the need of Speech

Do not wait for things to get easier, simpler, better. Life will always be complicated. Learn to be happy right now. Otherwise, you will be out of time.

Specific and viable solutions to the problems raised in

the previous step are presented to the audience.Introduce your solution. How will you solve the problem that your audience is now ready to address? This is the main part of your presentation. It will vary significantly, depending on your purpose. In this section:

- Discuss the facts.
- Elaborate and give details to make sure the audience understands your position and solution.
- Clearly state what you want the audience to do or believe.
- Summarize your information from time to time as you speak.
- Use examples, testimonials, and statistics to prove the effectiveness of your solution.
- Prepare counterarguments to anticipated objections.

Highly Effective Public Speaking Skills

- Statement will tell your audience in a very specific, direct sentence what it is you want them to do
- Explain what exactly it is you are advocating.
- Theoretical Demonstration: This is where you make it clear how what you are advocating fulfills the need you built
- Reference to Practical Experience: This is where you bring in external evidence supporting the value of your proposal.
- Meeting Objections: here you anticipate counter-arguments and you pre-empt them, i.e., address them before the audience has time to actually bring them up.
- Satisfaction Everyone needs to be responsible and accountable
- Background Habits form over time.
- Facts Introduce more statistics relevant to your topic
- Position Statement When workers are responsible and accountable for one another, safety compliance increases.
- Examples Present one or more case studies.
- Counterarguments

Skill No.13

Visualize the future

"Visualize your success then take action."

The solution is then described in such a way that the audience can visualize both the solution and its positive effects in a detailed manner. You can use three methods to help the audience share your vision:

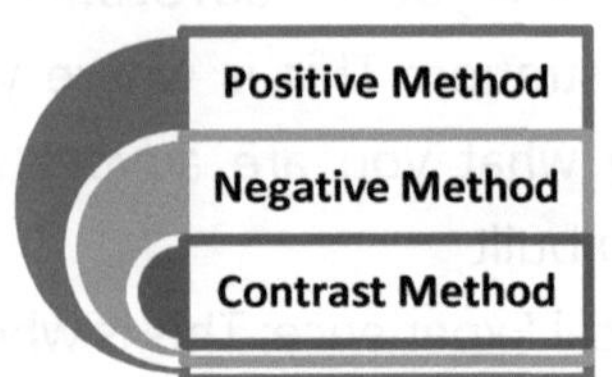

- ✓ Positive method Describe what the situation will look like if your ideas are adopted. Emphasize the positive aspects.
- ✓ Negative method Describe what the situation will look like if your ideas are rejected. Focus on the dangers and difficulties caused by not acting
- ✓ Contrast method Develop the negative picture first and then reveal what could happen if your ideas are accepted.
- ✓ In the consideration of the attentive step, you will likely get your audience paying attention to you. This is the work of the snare. In the need step, your goal is to establish a clear problem, and a clear problem that is directly relevant to your audience.

Skill No.14

Call for Action

"Words may inspire but only action creates change."
— Simon Sinek

The capacity of the activity step is to interpret the goal made in the Visualization Step into unmistakable activity and actionable step. It is the ideal opportunity for activity; clarify details with the audience, precisely what the speaker needs from them to do perform now and precisely how to do it. Public Speaker is making it simple for the audience to make a quick Move or quick action.

1. An appeal or challenge
2. Summary to the audience
3. Appropriate quotation

The Motivated Sequence Pattern is need base for strategy speeches that look for sure quick action. This characterization follows the course of human thought process and leads the audience systematically to the ideal activity. The crowd or audience is then advised how to tackle the issue utilizing the solution(s) recently presented.

Skill No.15

The objectives to prepare the speech

Objectives are not fate; they are direction. They are not commands; they are commitments..~Peter Drucker

Story:-Two grains were lying next to each other on the fertile rich soil. The first grain said: "I need to grow up I want to settle into the ground and sprout from the ground. I dream to blossom in delicate buds and proclaim the coming of spring. I want to feel the warm rays of the sun and dewdrops on my petals!".This grain grew up and turned into a delightful flower. The subsequent second grain said: "I'm scared, apprehensive. If I will put down my roots into the ground, I do not know what they will face there. If I will grow tender stems, they can be damaged by wind. In addition, if there will be flowers, they may be disrupted. Therefore, I would rather wait for a safer time.

The story is straightforward, correct. On the off chance that you have your dream in your psyche, accomplish something with it. The principal little advance you take will have an incredible effect.

Skill No.16

Nervousness is Normal. Practice and Prepare!

"In my nervousness for this speech and my moments of doubt, I've told myself firmly, 'if not me, who? If not now, when?'-Emma Watson"

All individuals feel some physiological reactions like high heart beating and shivering hands. Try not to connect these sentiments with the feeling that you will perform ineffectively. A nervousness is acceptable for some extent. The adrenaline surge that makes you sweat additionally makes you more ready and prepared to give your best performance.

"Practice makes perfect. After a long time of practicing, our work will become natural, skilful, swift and steady.- Bruce Lee"

The ideal way of conquering tension is to be in continuous preparation. Whenever you have become all right with the material, practice—a great deal. Tape yourself, or get a companion to evaluate your performance.

Skill No.17

Voice modulation

It only takes one voice, at the right pitch, to start an avalanche - Dianna Hardy

The voice is the most important to become a public speaker. The dictionary meaning of the word 'modulation' when referred to as voice implies regulating the voice as per the necessity of your speech. In this way, you must bring in a change in pace, pause, and pitch while speaking. Without modulation, your speech will be flat and monotonous.

The Outcome of Voice Modulation:

There would be a lot more advantages of voice modulation, yet these three should be recollected with the goal that you would consistently attempt to achieve a very much-balanced speech.

The accompanying three objectives are critical.

1) To empower the audience with a Complete understanding
2) To empower you to communicate your thoughts, ideas, message adequately.
3) To guarantee that you are not monotonous or talkative.

Tips to improve and practice the voice modulation

1. **Be loud and clear:** Being loud does not imply that you as a speaker need to shout at a high pitch. Ensure that your voice does not squeak while being noisy. This can bother/disturb the crowd and cause them to lose interest.

2. **Practice Variation:** You can look up certain means through which you can practice modulation. Work on talking with varieties in your speech. Let us recollect the past when we used to sing rhymes and tell stories of teachers. Keep in mind. Just the variation in your tone can convey your expression.

3. **Emphasize important words:** Words do not have an effect except if they are appropriately conveyed. You can take the optimum pauses and successful stops; weigh on a specific arrangement of words, which will help your speech sound more intuitive.

4. **Make an audience-pleasing Speech:** To connect with the audience, as a speaker, you might apply quotations, friendly talk, stories, etc. Exactly when you begin the speech. You can even see the value in them for being a decent crowd, or ask them a couple of inquiries with the goal that it draws you nearer to them. Engage your crowd with a story that they can relate to.. Describing excess stories will just occupy them.

5. **Powerful Pauses:** Pauses during a speech are vital. It creates interest, psychological curiosity in the mindsets of the audience. Ensure the speaker does not take extremely long stops, exhausting the crowd all things considered. **There are two viable stops:**

1. A pause just after your presentation.
2. A respite while moving to start with one topic to the next.

6. **Keep away from ahas and Uhms:** This can truly bother the crowd while paying attention to the speaker, on the off chance that he will in general continue to add fillers like Ahas and uhms repeatedly. To keep away from such fillers, you need to work on talking a lot.

7. **Sound Enthusiastic and Confident:** The crowd is looking for a legend in you when you are talking. Try not to sound junky, dull, or utilize a similar variety of tones in your speech. Show energy in a way that would sound natural to you.

8. **Speak moderately:** Another thing to be kept in mind is to speak moderately while delivering a speech! Speaking in a moderately and composed manner helps get your point across to your audience. So remember to speak moderately and clearly.

Skill No.18

Audience Relations

A great relationship is about two things, first, find out the similarities, second, and respect the differences.

Highly effective speakers will give priority to the professional respect and relations with audience. Acknowledge your participants/audience the immediate moment when you reach the stage. This helps the speaker to be more similar to a "genuine" individual and keeps a conversational tone.

- ✓ **Attention-grabbing immediately**, the point when you speak, the speaker will have around 60 seconds to catch public attention.
- ✓ **Friendly facial expression**. There will undoubtedly be friendly individuals in the audience. Identify those individuals and imagine that you are speaking to just them.
- ✓ **Effective eye contact.** Despite how huge your audience is, ensure the significant eye-to-eye connection with however many individuals as could reasonably be expected. It will cause them to feel like you are speaking straightforwardly to them.

Skill No.19

Improve your Language

Changes in Language often reflect the changing values of a culture- Ravi Zacharias

Learning and practicing the language will be an advantage in speakers' profiles. It enjoys benefits to

Widen Employment Prospects, Explore the World with Confidence, Access World-Class Education Systems, and Establishments, Increase Cognitive Ability, Start a Life in an English-Speaking Country, Improve Communication Skills, Open up a World of Entertainment and Popular Culture, Improve Your Confidence. The inquiry comes, what are the tips to work on your language? Scarcely any significant hints are reference base

1. Learn and practice one word each day: Pick a word you might want to chip away at and use practice it in various sentences. Utilize the word until you have learned it and continue to utilize it consistently.
2. Watch English movies and News bulletins: Watch films in English and focus on new vocabulary and articulation. Impersonate the entertainers and mess around with them.

3. Make companions Associate with English speakers or others willing to learn and communicate in English. Talk about things that you have learned and the transformation of ideas.
4. Practicing English language learning techniques: Take a cooking or any other interesting course in English or join a book club! Anything you appreciate doing, ensure you do it and impart it in English. Utilizing English to discuss things you appreciate will make rehearsing a positive encounter.
5. Have a discussion and debates: Discussion and debates on every one of the topics that interest you with your friend's circle in English. Attempt to use however much vocabulary that you can to make yourself clear and pay attention to different contentions cautiously so you can contend against them adequately.
6. Use a word reference in the Dictionary: Online dictionaries will provide word references regularly have sound models on your cell phone. However, try not to turn out to be too dependent on this mobile instrument.
7. Do not be hesitant to commit errors but ensure they should not repeat them: The public speaker's first objective is to convey a clear message to the audience. The secondary will be language, but it may not talk amazing English, with the right syntax and vocabulary.

8. Think in English: Go from speaking English to extraordinary English by thinking in the language. Initial learning you will find it troublesome to expertise in English from the get-go, but after some time you will figure out how to switch between speaking English and your first language.

9. Self-Talk: It will look like joking talking to self, we know. In any case, by conversing with yourself in English in front of the mirror for a couple of moments every day, you will realize when and how to utilize various articulations. You will likewise realize where you commit the majority of the errors.

10. Optimum utilization of Technology: A cell phone can be an incredible asset for learning dialects. Use it to record yourself speaking then, at that point, tune in back to perceive how your English sounds to others. Capitalize on the entirety of your cherished usefulness applications to sort out your practice time and make a note of the multitude of new words you learn.

11. Listen: Pay attention to news bulletins and songs in English to pay attention to the way to produce the words. You can likewise learn new

words and articulations along these lines. The more you tune in, the more you learn! Take imitation of what you hear to practice your articulation and realize which words in a sentence are worried.

12. Read English loud for all to hear

Eagerly read an English newspaper or a leading magazine out to yourself. You could even discover specific content for your cherished TV show and act it out! This in common is an extraordinary way of rehearsing articulation since you just need to focus on ensuring your English sounds incredible and do not have to stress over sentence construction or punctuation.

Skill No.20

Select a speech theme

Small minds can never handle great themes ~ St Jerome

A great speech starts with a great topic. It is so important that you select a topic that interests you, and you believe will interest your audience this might appear to be a simple undertaking, yet there are limitless public talking themes. How would you pick the right one? How would you choose a subject, which is an ideal fit among you and your crowd? Your subject prompts your core message — the whole presentation plans to convey this core message to your audience.

SEVEN STEPS TO PICK A PERFECT SPEECH TOPIC

Stress – the nervousness is on! You are beginning at a blank paper and you are clueless about what to discuss! This is the truth for such countless maturing and surprises to the speakers.

Prior to composing any speech choosing the right speech topic can be challenging. Effective public speaking is the Life guide on how to choose a speech topic and impart successfully. It might be in meetings, events, motivational talking or any other occasions.

Stage 1: IDENTIFY THE NATURE OF THE SPEAKING EVENT AND PURPOSE BEHIND IT

Discovering what the idea of the speaking occasion is and the main role behind it can truly help in reducing a theme, which is applicable and fit for reason. It might appear to be hard to miss yet there are speakers who get found out by setting up a speech they believe is on a reasonable point just to discover minutes before conveyance that the speech theme won't hit the imprint. Try not to make a wild presumption and know this fundamental data from the beginning. It can save shame in front of an audience and can truly assist thin with bringing down your quest for the right subject.

Stage 2: KNOW YOUR AUDIENCE

You may not have the foggiest idea about a solitary personality when you stand up before a specific audience however; there are shared traits between the people that make up any audience. This can be pretty much as basic as the one motivation behind why they are on the whole sitting in a similar room paying attention to you. Normal attributes can incorporate however are not restricted to – age, sexual orientation, convictions, status, instruction, leisure activities, experience, identity, and work. Monitoring the shared characteristics of your audience can help with choosing a point that is significant.

Stage 3: THINK OF YOUR PERSONAL INTERESTS, KNOWLEDGE, AND EXPERIENCES

Here comes the great part! It is currently about you as the speaker. Remembering the idea of the speaking occasion and your audience, what important points are of individual interest to you? As a speaker in case you are truly intrigued by your speech subject, it makes investigating, composing, and conveying it a lot more agreeable. What subjects do you as of now have information on and additionally have you had encounters that your audience can gain from? During this progression, the conceptualizing is kicking in and the thoughts are beginning to sway up to the surface.

Stage 4: IDENTIFY ANY RELEVANT LATEST NEWS

Picking the right point implies it should be applicable. Importance implies it should be current. Has there has been a blast of media on a specific subject that is important to both you and your audience? Doing some, general examination now can help extraordinarily in recognizing important subjects that are at the bleeding edge of the personalities of those in the audience that you find fascinating. During this examination interaction, it may be the case that you may not recognize an all-encompassing subject and you may stagger over supporting realities/stories/thoughts that help with driving the theme determination process.

Stage 5: BRAINSTORM ALL POSSIBLE IDEAS

To storm, a mind, it must be balanced by what can't be it must be challenged

With your research organization, brimming with a scope of thoughts it is time presently to conceptualize and archive every one of your thoughts regardless of how wild or crazy any of them might appear. Reporting all your subject thoughts is incredible in guaranteeing all prospects have been thought of. It very well might be useful at this stage to bob your thoughts another person as discussing them can frequently prompt considerably more subject thoughts that you may somehow not distinguish. There is no hard or quick standard with respect to what number point thoughts you ought to have yet your restriction in many cases is generally time.

Stage 6: MAKE A SHORT LIST OF POSSIBLE TOPICS

The secret of getting on the shortlist is doing your best work fearlessly for a long time before you get on the list.
~Seth Godin

Here comes time to take care of business. Presently the time has come to audit the rundown and tight it down to three theme finalists. Consider every one of the components in the means above and be heartless. Your thoughts are the most applicable to the speaking occasion. Which thoughts are probably going to be generally interesting to your audience? Which subject do you think generally about and discover fascinating? Are there any recent debated issues that will undoubtedly be a group pleaser? At this stage, you wanted to go with your gut impulse and not go through hours of discussion.

Stage 7: MAKE A DECISION AND COMMIT TO IT

A choice presently should be made and afterward you really wanted to adhere to it. At the point when you survey your short rundown of finalists, there might be one theme that simply jumps out at you, you end up normally holding with it and the speech is starting to think of itself to you. At the point when this happens, you have hit the big stake and the speech composing cycle can begin. However, in case you are battling to settle on a nail gnawing choice, one suggestion is to draft a general speech diagram list item style for every one of the short-recorded themes. While recognizing the central issues in the body of every speech diagram, the theme that is the simplest and the fastest to make is in all probability the one you think generally about and track down the most fascinating!

Pic :Bharatha Ratna Shri.Sardar Vallbahi Patel addressing the Public gathering

Skill No.21

Sincerity, Enthusiasm, Confidence, and Simplicity (SECS)

"Effort and courage are not enough without purpose and direction.-John F. Kennedy"

A decent topic not only interests your audience. Selecting a topic will be based on the Four Elements of Public Speaking with Sincerity, Enthusiasm, Confidence, and Simplicity (SECS) you will become a highly effective public speaker. Selecting a good topic will give a far way in giving these characteristics, capacities.Remember that your speech will be delivered to an audience. Overall, your audience will be engaged feeling you present their own topic. Increasing the likelihood by the audience is very important and SECS will lead to improving the probability that you accomplish your speech's motivation.

Explanation of SECS as follows

Sincerity :A speaker should be sincere, one needs to speak and effective communication with any audience – regardless of whether it is one individual or thousands. A decent theme will assist you with being sincere. Sincerity implies various things; it implies being transformative and honest with your audience, it implies you trust and believe will be of interest and advantage to your audience. In the event that, truth be told the speaker is not being honest and you do not actually believe in what you are communicating this will immediately end.

Genuine Sincerity opens people's hearts, while manipulation causes them to close."Daisaky Lkeda

Enthusiasm

Nothing great was ever achieved without enthusiasm. -Ralph Waldo Emerson

A speaker should have a credible enthusiasm and self-interest in what it is you need to speak with the audience. Enthusiasm is the fuel that inspires the audience to lead towards, being more productive, more positive, and more confident. Reinforcing confidence puts us in a position to better deal with fear, worry, and stress. Enhances motivation.

Confidence

"Your success will be determined by your own confidence and fortitude" - Michelle Obama.

It is a fearless trait of an effective speaker. An effective speaker should be persuaded that what you say is genuine, true, facts, that it merits saying, and that will fulfil the vision and mission of the purpose. The speaker should be sure that you know your subject and perform accordingly. Having personal power. Feeling valued. Decreasing negative/destructive thoughts.

Simplicity

"Simplicity is the soul of efficiency"~Austin Freeman

Speaker must consider his speech should be simple, expressive and logical. The message should not be unambiguous, forthright, and understandable. Selecting a good theme, you are an expert and perform, will help you to reach the message to the audience.

Skill No.22

Make a speech layout

Good Visual layout shows the logical structure of program.
~ Steve MacDonnell

To impart effective public speaking skills structure of speech layout plays a very important role to impact the audience. Without structure, the audience will either think about what is the core message is or they will lose interest in you altogether. Tragically, this progression is regularly jumped to "save time.

Following points to be considered while making speech layout

- ✓ Start with a greeting
- ✓ Begin your speech with attention focal point
- ✓ Give an option to the audience a valid reason for your speech
- ✓ Present your statement
- ✓ Establish your credibility
- ✓ Preview your main points

Skill No.23

Speech Writing Skills

"The art of writing is the art of discovering what you believe "~Gustave Flaubert

Speech composing is an iterative interaction that starts with your first draft. A temporarily uncooperative mind can disable speakers at this stage. The fourth article in the series examines how you can keep away from that snare to compose your first speech draft.

When the main draft is made, speech composing includes iteratively rubbing your speech into its best structure. Holding your conscience under control, you are well informed to alter pitilessly. The fifth article in the series tells you the best way to alter your speech for centre, clearness, concision, coherence, assortment, and effect.

Recollect that speeches ought to be composed for the ear; receiving metaphors will hold your speech back from seeming like an article or authoritative report.

Skill No.24

Apply gestures

The people who succeed are not the ones who avoid failure; they are the ones who learn how to respond to failure with optimism.

Gestures are very important. The motion will give a

replica to the audience that you do not have any stage fear and you are addressing them in a professional and friendly manner. If you tie your hands on stage, it gives a message you are having stage fear. *On top of your voice projection, the certainty of self- confidence level and capacity to empower the audience, hand gestures can help your speech and makes the audience more interested in the thing you are saying.*

- ✓ Hand gestures, can assist to make the talking environment dynamic. With these gestures, different talkers can know your feelings.
- ✓ This can make the discussion easily. Hand gestures can assist to others with understanding speaker core points rapidly.
- ✓ A great talk utilizes their gestures to tell the audience 'this is the main thing I need to say '. Hand gestures or body gestures can help you talk smoothly with the audience who communicate in different dialects.

Skill No.25

Practice

"Practice makes perfect. After a long time of practicing, our work will become natural, skill full, swift and steady." - Bruce Lee

Highly effective speakers appear to be professionals when they talk, nearly as if they are talking the words interestingly.

Practicing your speech makes you an expert of the substance. Requesting criticism and following up on it gives you the certainty that your presentation will be a success. Public speaking, similarly to some other abilities, requires consistent practice to be improved. The more you talk in public, the more you train your brain and body to perceive speaking as a natural and safe situation, the more certain you will feel at the centre of attention.

Rehearsing your speech ten, twenty, and surprisingly multiple times before the real speaking commence. It will make your presentation look significantly more natural, spontaneous characteristic and easy. Obviously, practice alone will not really make your performance calm, yet rehearsing your speech at any two or multiple times before the presentation holds three Significant Benefits:

- It permits you to practice tongue twisters that are difficult to see when you initially compose your speech.
- It will help to decrease the nervousness and assist with changing tension into energy upon the arrival of the presentation.
- It encourages you to measure your planning.

Practice alone

Prior to rehearsing and practicing your speech, it very well may be a smart thought to get ready "prompt" cards. The sign cards may contain the significant level speech components referenced in your blueprint, just as change phrases, watchwords, measurement information, or climaxes that you need to impart to your audience. Numerous public speaking books inform new speakers' practice in front of a mirror.

Practice before others

Speaking in front of the audience like family, friends will make overcoming stage fear.

Continuously take feedback; it might look for criticism from your audience toward the finish of a presentation. Request their assessment on themes, for example,

- How persuading and coherent your speaking was
- How fascinating, interesting, valuable and clear various pieces of your presentation were
- How well you addressed inquiries toward the finish of your speech
- What was their general impression of your performance
- Listen objectively specific to the audience feedback instead of take any suggestions or observations as personal criticism.

Do the last dress practice

A portion of the focus to consider while practicing your presentation:

- Will your audience have the option to see your presentation without any problem? They can see the presentation easily. Will you need to utilize a device microphone or not?
- Is there a spot to put your notes?
- What electronic gadgets are given (for an example LCD projector, screen, and amplifier) and what do you need to carry with you?

Skill No.26

Be passionate & enjoy yourself.

People with great passion can make the impossible happen

Great Passion is a win-win mutually beneficial characteristic for introductions; the audience wins by

getting a greater quality encounter, and the speaker's wins also by conveying an effective show. Pick a point on something critical to you, and that you have an enthusiastic outlook on. Your obligation to the subject will assist with offering the speech to your audience.

Enthusiasm and passion are both legitimate and charming. The earnestness of feeling shows up in nonverbal discussion. Presentations that incorporate representations that are novel are more critical and drawing in than introductions that are loaded up with unsurprising illustrations and pictures.

Skill No.27

Story Telling

"Storytelling is the most powerful way to put ideas into the world today" ~Robert McKee

The best stories to use in your public speech may include verifiable realities from your life; self-destroying amusing realities about your previous oversights, and difficulties; examples of overcoming adversity from celebrated individuals' accounts; and stories that investigate the historical backdrop of your business.

Do's and Don'ts of Storytelling

Few out of every odd story will catch your audience's eye and interest. There are a couple of significant focuses that ought to be contemplated while picking the correct story for your speech:

Do's

- ✓ Always make your story applicable to the current subject
- ✓ Keep your stories simple and short

- ✓ Eliminate immaterial detail
- ✓ Space stories at spans to reemphasize your message
- ✓ Make sure the strategy of the story includes an exercise or a change result that your audience members can identify with and advantage from.
- ✓ Use proper non-verbal communication and outward appearances to pass on feelings to your audience members.
- ✓ Use components of the story that your audience can identify with (for example individuals, spots, and recognizable realities).
- ✓ Emphasize the descriptors and action words in your stories to make them sound intriguing.
- ✓ Learn your stories by heart

Don'ts

- Do not utilize more than a few stories on a similar theme as each progressive one will lose its effect
- Do not use terms that are unfamiliar to the experience of the audience
- Do not fill stories with such a large number of characters, occasions or subtleties.

Skill No.28

Body language

"Effective communication is 20% what you know and 80%how you feel about what you know. Jim Rohn"

Body language is non-verbal correspondence that incorporates motions, postures, and the development movements we make. It is usually something we do not think about when we are talking or presenting. No matter the speaker is making interesting or engaging a speech if the speaker is projecting negative body language gestures then the audience is less likely to listen to what they're saying. Lift your communication abilities with our verbal communication courses

The following are 6 methods for utilizing these signals to enable and connect with your understudies.

1. Eye to eye connection

Perhaps the ideal method for associating with our audience. Your audience is probably going to focus closer when they realize you are speaking straightforwardly to them. It likewise assists them with feeling seen.

2. Be Expressive and Use Gestures

Move understudies to become engaged with the example. Snare their minds. Standards for dependability are falling short on verbal material yet increment when you include noteworthy nonverbal prompts for the mind to document as an affiliation.

3. Keep Your Arms Open

An open body position signals a greeting. It invites conceptualizing and novel thoughts.

4. Praise your body

Gesture your head. Offer a go-ahead possibly two! Lift your hands in fervour. Show them they are on the correct way and they will be more certain about proceeding down it.

5. Practice a Thinking Pose

Hold your jaw, slant your head. This will move toward the understudy you are looking at to contemplate the inquiry. It rouses interest.

6. Presentable smile

This is the most significant. Audience as associated best with speech who need to be available with them, who love learning, and who need to share that enthusiasm.

Being more aware of nonverbal correspondence in the audience will permit us to become viable communicators of information.

Here are the absolute most normal kinds of body language to pay special mind to:

Very aggressive

- An excessively strong handshake.
- Attacking individual space.
- Hands-on hips or legs excessively wide.
- Staring eye contact
- Physical aggressive movements

Cautious

- Crossed arms or legs.
- An absence of eye-to-eye connection.
- Inclining ceaselessly.
- Slouched shoulders.
- Eye rolls.

Anxious or Nervous

- Gnawing nails.
- Squirming.
- Hacking.
- Weak Feeble handshake.
- Putting hands on head.

Skill No.29

Professional appearance

"No matter how you feel getup, dress up show up and never give up"~Regina Brett

The first impression is "A picture is worth a thousand words." Remember this when getting ready to meet with a planned boss. Appropriate grooming and a professional appearance are key importance to yield respect to the audience. The manner in which you look and conduct yourself makes an impact on individuals you work close by.

Follow appropriate grooming techniques

- Try To Wear Clean And Presentable Clothes
- Some fundamental rules to keep are:
- Be spotless and perfect, including your fingernails, teeth, shoes, hair and face
- The professional two-piece matching suit in a normal colour
- Empty pockets-no bulges or tinkling coins/keys, etc.
- No gum, candy or cigarettes
- Do not interrupt and do not argue!
- Don't chew gum

ITEM	GROOMING
Hair	Clean, trimmed and neatly combed or arranged.
Facial Hair (men)	Freshly shaved; mustache or beard neatly groomed.
Fingernails	Neat, clean, and trimmed.
Teeth	Brushed and fresh breath
Breath	Beware of foods. Beware of tobacco, alcohol, and coffee odor. Use a breath mint if needed.
Body	Freshly bathed/showered; use deodorant. Remove body piercings, tongue rings, and cover tattoos if possible.
Make-up (Women)	Use sparingly and be natural looking.

Skill No.30

Speech Pace

A speech should not just be a sharing of Information, but a sharing of yourself. ~Ralph Arch bold

The pace of the speech is the speed at which we say our considerations for all to hear. Often when individuals feel anxious or energized, nervous they will be in a general hurry through their conveyance, expecting to get the presentation over as fast as could be expected.

Experienced public speakers often differ their speed during a presentation to hold their audience's consideration throughout an extensive stretch of time and add zest to their speech. However, the greatest piece of a presentation ought to be conveyed at a rate that permits your audience members to get a handle on your message and let it hit home.

Skill No.31

Pitch

The right word may be effective nothing has ever been as effective as a rightly named Pause

Pitch is an arrangement of voice. Variety of voice pitches during the presentation. Fluctuating your voice in pitch during a presentation is the most straightforward approach to:

- ✓ Avoid tedium and hold the audience's advantage
- ✓ Add tone and energy to the speech
- ✓ Make certain words and thoughts stick out
- ✓ Appear loose and sure to the audience members

While setting up your speech, it is imperative to recognize and take note of the specific words or expressions that you might want to relate to your audience members to recollect. For instance, you may utilize a higher pitch voice for fervour and a lower pitch to add weight and earnestness to the message.

Skill No.32

Core message

If your core message is not delivered clearly and unequivocally, then it may be misinterpreted or misunderstood. ~ Peter Dhu

Your core message is the focal thought of your presentation. All other presentation speech components should uphold the core message.

- Clarity: Aim to communicate & express your core message in a solitary sentence. In the event that you cannot do this, you need greater clearness.
- Passion: Your centre message should be something you have faith in.
- Knowledge / Information: What do you think about this core message? Would you be able to draw stories from individual experience? Have you investigated the theme?

Speaker believe that whole presentation will be remember. Actually, the audience will hold just a couple of focuses. Your speech should be intended to guarantee that your audience remember your core message.

Skill No.33

Composing for Impact the speech to the audience.

Good composition is like a suspension bridge each line adds strength and takes none away. ~Robert Henri

The research of way of talking/rhetoric furnishes speechwriters with various rhetorical devices. Of the enormous number of rhetorical devices, explore in three segments:

- ✓ Devices which include sounds (frequently with repetition) for example similar sounding word usage, sound similarity, sound to word imitation
- ✓ Devices which include repetition of Ideas, expressions, (frequently with parallelism)
- ✓ Devices that change the standard significance of words i.e. usual meaning

Skill No.34

Prompt Communication

Punctually is not about being on Time, It is about respecting your known commitments.

Keep a culture of straightforwardness with your client. Be straightforward to share genuine data. Trustworthiness consistently brings rewards, and that would be the greatest benefit for you over others.

Give right and exact data to your audience. Try not to keep your client hanging tight for a reaction. Everybody loves prompt reactions. Make yourself refreshed about ongoing communications, progressed procedures, successful instruments, and late news.

- ✓ Present with certainty
- ✓ Keep in touch with their audience members
- ✓ Precisely present inside a given time span
- ✓ Recollect their speaking focuses in general
- ✓ Recount statements and specialized measurements exactly.
- ✓ Enhance their picture by making themselves clear really.

Skill No.35

SMART Speech Preparation

It's not that i am so smart, it's just that i stay with problems longer ~ Albert Einstein

It is part of every aspect of presentation a sense of direction, motivation, a clear focus, and clarify importance.
SMART is an acronym that stands for

- Specific
- Measurable
- Achievable
- Realistic
- Timely.

Therefore, SMART preparation increases the chances of achieving speaking and presentation with great success.

S= SPECIFIC
To make a goal specific, the five "W" questions must be considered:

- Who: Who is involved in this goal?
- What: What do I want to accomplish?
- Where: Where is this goal to be achieved?
- When: When do I want to achieve this goal?
- Why: Why do I want to achieve this goal?

M=Measurable

A SMART preparation is measuring progress with certain criteria. To make a goal measurable, ask yourself:

- How many/much?
- How do I know if I have reached my goal?
- What is my indicator of progress?

A= Achievable

A SMART goal must be achievable and attainable. Ask yourself:

- Do I have the resources and capabilities to achieve the goal? If not, what am I missing?
- Have others done it successfully before?

R=Realistic

A SMART goal must be realistic in that the goal can be realistically achieved given the available resources and time. Question yourself Ask yourself:

- Is the goal realistic and within reach?
- Is the goal reachable, given the time and resources?
- Are you able to commit to achieving the goal?

Timely

A SMART goal must be time-bound in that it has a start and finish date. Question yourself:

- Does my goal of presentation have a deadline?
- By when do you want to complete goal?

What thoughts or ideas would you like to impart to your audience? How would you make your presentation paramount? What do you start with? A SMART Speech Preparation equation permits any speaker to conquer an inability to write and assemble an extraordinary presentation. A confident speaker can be thrown by unforeseen problems, especially when technology is involved.

If you are using audio-visual aids, try to have a plan B in case your laptop crashes or your Wi-Fi connection vanishes. If you are well prepared, tech problems will be one less thing to worry about.

Tips to preparation

- Do It the before time– Preparation the "day of" can help you get ready in advance. Even better, preparation the night before can help you remedy any shortfalls that may occur.

- Advance – The further in advance you prepare, the more time you have to remedy any unforeseen obstacles. Gather materials for that big event several days beforehand.

- Do the (Pre) Work – Preparation is about doing the work in advance. Read the materials. Review the data. Practice the activity. It is all about being ready.

- Save Time – Some will use the excuse that they do not have extra time to prepare in advance. Yet, preparing actually saves you time. It reduces errors, prevents re-work, and shortens activities. Properly prepared meetings take much less time to conduct.

- Reduce Your Stress – When you are ready, you are confident. When you are prepared, your stress is reduced because you have less to worry about.

- Make It a Habit – Make preparation part of your lifestyle, not something you do rarely. Preparation should be part of your daily habits.

Skill No.36

Time Management

Time is more valuable than money. You can get more money, but you cannot get more time. ~ Jim Rohan

In every aspect of life, time management is essential. We all know it in theory, but managing time effectively in practice can be difficult. As a result, there is a lot of time pressure on stage!

Here are five practical strategies for managing your time on stage every time:

- Know the time
- Practice the time
- Develop a healthy mind-set
- Not to mention the reference of Time
- Audience participation

Know the time.

It may appear simple, but many speakers take the stage

without a mechanism for keeping track of the time. There is no visible clock. Wearing a watch is the simplest and most effective way to avoid being caught off guard. Using your phone is also an option, but it is more clumsy and distracting than a watch. You have the best chance of succeeding if you know the time.

Have practice time.

A vital component of planning and rehearsing a speech appropriately before conveyance is to time it.

Develop a healthy mind-set

To develop from the limits featured above, having a solid attitude and healthy mind-set towards each public speaking experience will help altogether in accomplishing successful time management. Prior to venturing into the not really settled to partake in each second, have an arrangement set up to follow time during conveyance, and choose early to regard your audience's time by remaining on time!

Allow the audience to participate their time.

Allow the audience to have a good time. Effective time management is not about gaining as much information as possible into as little time as possible. It is all about knowing how to make the most of your time in order to provide a worthwhile and memorable experience for your audience.

Key benefits of the time management as follows

- ✓ Never miss cut-off times
- ✓ Become a genius at arranging
- ✓ Improve the Quality of Your Work
- ✓ Learn Prioritization
- ✓ Self-Confident
- ✓ Better Productivity
- ✓ Manage unwanted Interruptions
- ✓ Defeat Distractions
- ✓ Take Effective Decisions
- ✓ Boosts self-Efficiency
- ✓ Face Fewer less Team Conflicts
- ✓ Bring down Your Anxiety and Stress
- ✓ Forestall the Need to Rush
- ✓ Investigate New Learning Opportunities
- ✓ Strength self portrait

Skill No.37

Eliminate filler words.

The development of self-confidence starts with the elimination of this demon called fear ~ Napoleon Hill

Any meaningless noises, words, or phrases used by a speaker to fill in a pause or a gap during a speech are known as filler words. Although we never type these terms in print, practically every speaker uses them without even realizing it. Examples: Well /sum/Uh, Hmm, You know, Uh-uh. These seemingly innocuous words may appear to be just that. However, what is the harm in utilizing them? However, when someone uses it excessively, it might be for one of the following reasons:

- They themselves are not very sure of what they are saying.,They are lying because they have not practiced mentally rehearsed the message they wish to deliver.
- They just are not the best communicators verbally,They're in stress and nervous

Techniques to overcome the fillers

- ✓ Record yourself,
- ✓ Practice & slowdown your phase
- ✓ be normal in your speech
- ✓ Structure your speech
- ✓ Learn speech flows

Skill No.38

Take every opportunity to speak.

Every problem is an opportunity for a solution.

When you appear in front of an audience on a stage, you are immediately perceived as an authority and expert in your domain. More people want to collaborate with you if you are perceived as an expert. You begin to communicate/share your message with others. You begin to gain a reputation as a thinking leader. Simply speaking will urge others to want to collaborate with you.

Few tips and benefits are mentioned below

- ✓ Start early
- ✓ Livestream your talk
- ✓ Be social in that event
- ✓ Organize a post-session meetup
- ✓ Give and get follow-up info

Skill No.39

Mentally prepare.

Mentally prepare then physically dominate.

If you are going to give a speech, it is a good idea to mentally prepare before going onstage. Organizing your ideas before speaking will help you deliver an effective speech, whether you are speaking to five or fifty people.

Public speaking needs a great deal of mental preparation. To psychologically prepare, you should focus your attention on the audience and the message. Successful public speaking requires mindfulness and complete focus on the work at hand. Following tips will help psychologically to be mentally prepared for the successful public speaking

- ✓ Transform your speech into a story
- ✓ If you do not have much time to prepare, memories information.
- ✓ If you have to make a speech on a range of themes, organize your knowledge into categories.
- ✓ Build contingency plan
- ✓ Control your nervous system.
- ✓ Before you go onstage, try to avoid negative self-talk.

Skill No.40

Attend Other Presentations.

Every successful presentation is built on four pillars. People, Idea, Passion and Preparations. ~ Hasina K M

The successful speakers will learn from others and increase their own abilities and knowledge about your field if you attend other presentations. This demonstrates respect for your fellow speakers while also allowing you to gauge the audience's reaction. The key objectives to attend other presentations is mentioned below

- ✓ Get feedback on a draft of your most recent project.
- ✓ Meet new experts in your profession but also learn about the most recent research
- ✓ Improve your public speaking and communication abilities.
- ✓ Take a trip to a new location and have a good time.
- ✓ Get to know your intellectual leaders.
- ✓ Participate in high-level debates to improve your ideas.
- ✓ Increasing the value of your CV

Skill No.41

Knowledge

Knowledge is Power. Information is liberating. Education is the premise of progress, in every society, in every family.
~ Kofi Annan

In your job as a public speaker, it is critical that you are both proficient with regard to your topic and gifted in speaking procedures.

You could have the following questions:

- ✓ What kind of expertise and knowledge is required?
- ✓ What are the advantages of becoming a public speaker?
- ✓ How does a public speaker gain knowledge?

The key factors to increase the knowledge of the speaker is as follows

Expertise and knowledge

Being a competent speaker entails being well versed in both topic matter and delivery strategies. A speaker with little expertise does not understand what he or she is talking about or how to deliver an effective presentation. Speaking skills imply

that you have mastered speaking strategies and are capable of giving excellent Speaking skills imply that you have mastered speaking strategies and are capable of giving an excellent speech.

Knowledge and skill are part of the natural development in progression from good health, excellence, value, and honor.

Importance and advantages

It is much simpler to give a speech if you are well versed in the subject and have excellent speaking skills. Anxiety and shame might stem from a lack of information. A competent speaker gets a greater response from the audience.

A skilled platform speaker will know how to deliver a successful speech in a variety of situations and will be able to respond to unanticipated developments. Through his or her ability to talk, a competent speaker may frequently overcome a lack of information. Being knowledgeable and skillful reaps benefits such as confidence, esteem, and audience admiration.

Skill No.42

The context of your presentation

Without context words and actions have no meaning at all?
-Gregory Bateson

The public speaker should be knowledgeable about

his or her topic or subject and have outstanding public speaking abilities. Speaking with confidence and expertise boosts your confidence and raises listener attention. You may obtain information by studying and competence by putting what you have learned into practice.

Meaning is context bound, but context is boundless.
~Jonathan Culler

The context of a successful presentation will be having following key elements

- ✓ Immediate delivery
- ✓ Contrast and compare
- ✓ Use the appropriate words at the appropriate moment.
- ✓ Remove any unnecessary information.
- ✓ Establish your authority and communicate your ideals.
- ✓ Make an impression that will last.

Skill No.43

Three S -Stand. Settle. Smile.

Never go back for less, just because you are too impatient to wait for the best

When you take the stage, stand, settle in your place for a few seconds and then smile prior to speaking.

Standing

Standing in front of the audience was shown to be able to maintain their concentration / focus better and for longer than seated and giving speech. It shown that we think well while we are standing up - which is quite useful when giving a presentation. When delivering a presentation, it is natural to stand since it makes us feel more confident, in charge, and authoritative.

The advantages of giving a presentation while standing are as follows:

1. Positioning
2. Make eye contact
3. Vocal gestures
4. Facial expressions

Settle: Most of us have a period at the start of a speech when we are not present and confident, when we are not quite "in the groove."

Being settled entails two steps:

Feel your anxiousness first. For those of us who despise "bad" sentiments, this is more difficult than it appears

Now take a deep breath out gently. Allow the stress in your mind and body to dissipate as you do so.

Smile

Smiling makes, you feel more relaxed and relieves stress, which is especially beneficial when you are apprehensive about giving your speech. It draws a pleasant environment that enables for an engaged dialogue since it is contagious. It conceals your genuine feelings. Smiling hides your anxiety and makes you feel more upbeat.

Benefits

- ✓ It Improves Your Mood
- ✓ It has the ability to conceal your stress
- ✓ It Exhibits Self-confidence
- ✓ It Increases Audience Engagement Smiling is pleasant to the audience.
- ✓ It is contagious to smile.

Skill No.44

Prepare in bullet form.

Perhaps the best test of a man's intelligence is his capacity for making a summary. ~ Lytton Strachey

Start with essential words or phrases in bullet form if you can. Bullet points are still useful in presentations because, when utilized properly, they provide a variety of advantages to the audience.

Advantages

- ✓ Simple to interpret / understanding
- ✓ Give a general summary review
- ✓ There is strength in numbers.
- ✓ Compare and rank
- ✓ Simple and quick
- ✓ Options for simple animation
- ✓ Make use of animations.

Skill No.45

Concentration on Speech

Concentration is the root of all the higher abilities in man.
~ Bruce Lee

Concentration is about commitment and dedication to yourself. Keep your focus on your own goals and what is important to you, rather than distractions from outside source.Concentrate your speech, if you have written something in a previous draught that deviates from your main theme, edit it ruthlessly. Every point, every statistic, every anecdote, every tale, every joke, and every visual aid in your speech must reinforce your essential idea.Focus is a wonderful talent that comes with a lot of work and experience. All of one's mental energy is focused on one thing.

Objectives of Focus Presentation improves following skills

- ✓ Social Skills
- ✓ Communication has improved.
- ✓ Clarify and challenge preconceptions and conclusions.
- ✓ Discover ideas and concerns that may not have been considered at first, but are critical to the client.
- ✓ Figure out how you make decisions.

Skill No.46

Simple and clarity speech

Clarity of mind means clarity of passion, in addition; this is why a great and clear mind love ardently and sees distinctly what it loves. ~ Blaise Pascal

The attention span of today's audiences is extremely short, so the longer you speak, even if you are giving wonderful, engaging ideas, the more likely you are to lose their attention.

If your tale or points are not delivered, the message should be removed from your speech.

Steps to Make a Speech for shortness

- ✓ Delete any words that do not contribute to the meaning of the sentences.
- ✓ Long words should be replaced with short terms that are interchangeable.
- ✓ For instance, instead of using, you might use.
- ✓ A short speech is more likely to hold the attention of the audience.

Skill No.47

Momentum for Continuity

"Priority and continuity are the most important things to achieve your goals. ~Teja sree"

Speech should never be delivered in a continuous stream. Listeners can only make sense of speech by differentiating the components that make it up - words. If the material of a speech flows easily, the audience is more likely to pay attention.

The importance of momentum in delivering a good speech cannot be overstated. Information that is organized around a core idea, followed by essential points and various details, is easier to grasp. It also exhibits dependability and a thorough understanding of the topic.

Skill No.48

Uniqueness in speech

Be yourself. You are truly unique. There is something you can do better than anyone else.

Audiences are attracted to uniqueness. It increases the audience's delight in the speech while also allowing you to appeal to a variety of viewpoints. You must "stand out" as a speaker to be truly effective.

People want to know what distinguishes you from the rest of the pack. There is no quick fix for giving a fantastic speech. To become an excellent speaker, you must practice and be distinctive.

Being one of a kind, on the other hand, is a positive trait. "Consider if each component of your presentation is required. "Remove any information that isn't required."

Skill No.49

Speech Impact

Every action we take impacts the lives of others around us. The question is you aware of your impact. ~Arthur Carmazzi

Speech and language have an influence on the development of emotional and social capacities. Language and communication skills will be important for successful discourse.

There are several ways that are closely related to producing a memorable speech, including:

- ✓ Your performance should wow and surprise the audience.
- ✓ Create eye-catching images.
- ✓ Make a real effort to engage the senses.
- ✓ Make lines that people will remember for a long time.
- ✓ In your writing, use comparisons, similes, and idioms.
- ✓ Use rhetorical strategies throughout.

A life is not important except in the impact it has on other lives. ~ Jackie Robinson

Skill No.50

Monotone speeches should be avoided.

Vibes are always vibrant when blended with enthusiasm ~ The Inner voice

Shyness, fear of expressing emotions, or a lack of trust in your ability to alter your voice effectively can all contribute to a monotonous voice. If we do not put enough effort or attention into our speaking patterns, we may come off as monotonous.

- ✓ Breathe. If you do not have enough energy to support your voice, it is hard to talk with authority or presence.
- ✓ Stand up straight. Yes, your voice is influenced by your posture.
- ✓ Make a highlighter through your voice.
- ✓ Take a pause ,Narrate a story
- ✓ Have a conversation.
- ✓ Check and see if you have a monotone voice.
- ✓ Make a recording of your speech & listen to it.
- ✓ Improve your voice by using your body language.
- ✓ Allowing your voice to be emotive is something you should practise.
- ✓ Learn to feel at ease when expressing emotions.

Skill No.51

Do not hide from your audience.

You have nothing to fear, if you have nothing to hide.
~Joseph Goebbels

You miss any emotional relationship with the audience when you hide your feelings. When you properly communicate your emotion to the audience, on the other hand, your connection to the audience is highest.

- ✓ If you are feeling anything, show it. It's a basic concept
- ✓ Show your enthusiasm for your issue if you are passionate about it.
- ✓ Show your emotions if you are in sadness.
- ✓ Show your excitement to the audience if you are thrilled.
- ✓ Though you are ego, act as if you are self-assured.
- ✓ Show if you are thinking.
- ✓ Speakers are guilty of this all too frequently.

Skill No.52

Negative topics should avoided.

Negative thinking definitely attract negative results.
~Norman Vincent Peasle

Concentrate on positive or upbeat messaging. While it is occasionally important to address a bad subject, give constructive suggestions for how the problem might be addressed or remedied.

You cannot expect to live a positive life, if you hang with with negative people. ~ Jeel Osteen

Negative topics should be avoided wherever possible. Keep a close watch on the time. Negative people may take your attention even when you are not with them if you are not careful.

- ✓ Make a choice on how you want to feel.
- ✓ Your thoughts should be redirected.
- ✓ Make a conscious decision to operate in a positive manner.
- ✓ Seek out people who are excited about what they are doing.

For many, negative thinking is a habit, over time, becomes an addiction. Peter Mc Williams

Skill No.53

Speak about your requirements

Big results require big ambitions~James Champy

Speak out about your requirements. Expect no one to predict what you want from your audience, interviewer, or club. Be open and honest about your objectives.

Three main reasons for speaker should express the requirements/needs in public speaking texts: to

1. Inform
2. Convince
3. Amuse / entertain.

The obvious benefit of straightforward communication is that your message will be easily understood. The audience wants to know how you can assist them, but they do not want to spend hours trying to figure out what you are trying to say. Hence, express your clear intentions to the audience at optimum time.

Skill No.54

Audio record will improve your speech

We have so much access to video and audio recording equipment that it is kind of the new pen and paper
~ Hannah Hart

Take notes on what you have learned from the audio recordings. Many delivery features, such as speaking rate, pitch, and pauses, may be assessed using audio recordings.

- Determine which phrases sound "excellent" and which are difficult to understand.
- Filler words: Keep an ear out for ums, ahs, and other filler words.
- Keep track: of when and if you stumbled.

Time the entire speech as well as isolated chunks of the speech.

Skill No.55

Reciprocity between the speaker and the audience

There is one word, which may serve as a rule of practice for all ones life - Reciprocity. ~Confucius

Reciprocity offers to the Speaker and audience with "the functional practice of exchange matters with others for mutual benefit".Reciprocity is a powerful method for a speaker to gaining one's acquiescence with a request, as well as a major deciding element of human behaviour.

Types of Reciprocity

1. Positive Reciprocity
2. Negative Reciprocity

Positive reciprocity: It happens when the speaker's activity has a good impact on another person and is reciprocated with just an action that has a similar positive impact.Negative reciprocity: happens when an activity that has a negative impact of the speaker on the audience on someone is reciprocated with an action that has a negative impact on the same person.

Positive Reciprocity is the best practice that an effective public speaker will implement for his successful speech.

Skill No.56

Speech consistency across time

Consistency is what transform average into Excellence.
~Gymaholic

Why do people have such a difficult time staying consistent? Several variables might contribute to a person's difficulty to maintain consistency. The following are some examples:

- An unwillingness to wait.
- A great need for quick satisfaction.
- A lack of concentration and clarity.
- There aren't enough supporting behaviours or triggers

Characteristics that an excellent speaker should have in his personality

1. Consistency is how your worth is communicated.
2. Maintaining consistency gives you traction.
3. Maintaining consistency will aid your progress....
4. The key to having an impact is consistency!
5. Maintaining consistency gives you clarity and broadens your perspectives.

6. A perception of excellence is fostered through consistency.
7. Consistency leads to the formation of beneficial relationships.
8. It encourages self-discipline and self-control.
9. Consistency improves your self-esteem.
10. Consistency promotes progress; it earns you recognition; and it develops accountability.
11. Keeping a consistent schedule can help you stay motivated.
12. Maintaining Consistency
13. If you want to be more consistent and effective, consider the following suggestions.
14. Make a list of goals that you want to achieve.
15. Schedule time each week to focus on the things that matter to you.
16. Recognize your triggers and motivators.
17. Keep a frequent record of your progress and ask comments.

Skill No.57

Speaker with likable personality

It is better to be likable than to be talented. ~Utah Philips

Likeability is defined as having attributes that elicit positive feelings: pleasant, agreeable. Likeable traits are more likely to obtain support, love, aid, and caring from others, as well as the things they need. Look for yourself. How likely are you to reach out and help someone who has been cruel and unjust to you? It would be incredibly difficult to do.

The following are desirable attributes in a public speaker.

- ✓ There is not any ego.
- ✓ They are genuine and sincere.
- ✓ They provide us joy and provide us with a sense of security.
- ✓ Make a good first impression with your face.
- ✓ They give a great first impression.
- ✓ They establish a balance between zeal and pleasure.
- ✓ They give each other a warm grin.
- ✓ People are turned off by negativity.
- ✓ When describing other people, use favorable terms.
- ✓ People that are nice are often open-minded.

Skill No.58

Communication through Consensus

A consensus means that everyone agrees to say collectively what no one believes individually. ~Abba Eban

Consensus communication and decision-making is a method of gaining trust, ownership, and commitment. A successful consensus-building process is inclusive and involves all parties. Consensus choices may lead to higher-quality outcomes, allowing a group or community to go forward together to shape their future. Consensus communication is founded on the members of a group's mutual consideration and respect. It entails some consultation.Consensus decision-making has a number of advantages.

- ✓ Participation that is inclusive engages and empowers the group.
- ✓ It necessitates a commitment to collaborate and improves collaboration.
- ✓ Through debate, creates a shared understanding that bridges divisions.
- ✓ Equalizes power distribution in a group, allowing for better judgments

Skill No.59

Learn how to learn?

The capacity to learn is a gift, the ability to learn is a skill, and the willingness to learn is a choice. ~ Brain Herbert

Learning is a continuous process that encourages the development of skills, knowledge, and abilities in a variety of areas. Learning how to learn becomes much more important as the major source of information and knowledge. Learning aids in the development of critical thinking skills as well as the discovery of new ways to communicate with people from different cultures

Advantages of learning to learn for the Speaker is

- ✓ Boost your cognitive Psychological abilities.
- ✓ Make new friends.
- ✓ Participate in your community's activities.
- ✓ You should be pleased with your new talent.
- ✓ Have fun with it.
- ✓ Your rate of learning accelerates.
- ✓ You may build links between different skill sets.
- ✓ You become a more intriguing person because of this.
- ✓ It is anti-boredom.
- ✓ You are more adaptable to change.

Learn continually- there is always "one more thing" to learn ~ Steve Jobs

Skill No.60

Positivity is the direction for growth

"Train your mind to see the good in everything; Positivity is a choice. The happiness of your life depends on the quality of your thoughts."

For the speaker, to be clear, positive thinking does not imply that you are unaware of the negative aspects of life. It indicates that instead of grumbling about something, you strive to find a solution in a helpful way. We must battle depression, which is aided by optimistic thinking.

Following tips will help the speaker to improve positivity in their speech

- ✓ Not backward, but forwards enhanced living quality
- ✓ Passion, smile as if you mean it
- ✓ Consider positive ideas.
- ✓ Greater amounts of energy
- ✓ Enhanced mental and physical well-being
- ✓ Keep your expectations in check.
- ✓ Make a difference by recovering faster from an injury or sickness.
- ✓ Colds are less common.
- ✓ Find a hobby that you enjoy.
- ✓ Depression rates are lowest
- ✓ Stronger coping and stress management abilities

Skill No.61

Self-Recording videos

A video without a storyboard is like a house without a foundation ~ Han Lung

Do you make a variety of motions or do they all seem the same? Do you have a grin on your face? Are you fidgeting or behaving in any other distractible ways? Do you find yourself swaying from side to side?

The solution is to practice video recording and learn to overcome video recording of oneself speaking may be a very effective tool. All of your habits are recorded, both good and negative. You can also learn: in addition to the audio evaluations.

With a video recording of the curriculum, the student may spend more time on the section of the course that they do not understand learning and relearning the subject until they do. This is a highly zed learning method that allows students to study at their own speed and in their own time.

Advantages

1. Improves speaking skills
2. Prevents Perception Distortion
3. Increases Practice Efficiency
4. Lessons are improved
5. Encourages objectivity

Skill No.62

Stop taking things personally right away

Try not to take things personally. What people say about you is a reflection of them, not you.

Do not take things too seriously. If the issue is

contentious, your audience may have strong feelings about it. Consider their comments instructive. However, criticism is unavoidable in life, and the ability to receive sensible negative comments without overreacting is a valuable life skill.

Not only can we avoid feeling wounded or disgraced if we can hear legitimate criticism of our conduct without taking it personally, but we also avoid criticism increasing. Examine your own sense of excellence. Stop being so concerned with what others think of you.

Tips to make an effort not to take it personally

- ✓ Maintain control of your emotions
- ✓ Consider the criticism
- ✓ Allow yourself some leeway
- ✓ Show your gratitude
- ✓ Exhibit humility.
- ✓ Apologize in a cautious manner
- ✓ Do not get caught up in the criticism.

Skill No.63

Ask thought-provoking question to your audience.

There are three types of people in this world
Those who make things happen,Those who watch thing happen and Those who wonder what happened.

Obtain the attention of the audience by introducing a question to which they may or may not have an answer. Pose probing questions to the audience. It is tough for you to judge your speech's development and acceptability from the perspective of your audience since you know your message so well.

- ✓ When you are practicing, ask your practice audience clear testing questions like, what was the most crucial message?
- ✓ What was the most important message if something went wrong?
- ✓ If they answer with anything that is not in line with the message you delivered, you have a problem.
- ✓ Is it evident that the communication was received?
- ✓ Were there any words, phrases, or components that stumped you?
- ✓ Did it make contact with you?

Skill No.64

Fluency in Language / speech

Fluency is smooth, rapid, effortless use of language David Crustal

The use of written language in superior communication is significantly less common than most people imagine. Our words are only accountable for 7% of our discourse. Our nonverbal language (the other 93%) is influenced by our gestures and animation (38%) as well as our posture or body language (55 percent). It is vital to understand how to employ and emphasise these nonverbal. As much as possible, unwind.

- ✓ Make an emotional connection with your audience.
- ✓ Prepare your speech in advance and speak with zeal.
- ✓ a directness of perception a fervent outburst
- ✓ Physical strength
- ✓ Some myths have been disproved.
- ✓ Only extroverts have the ability to do so.

Languages have never been a strong suit of mine, and English is not my first tongue. A few myths have been disproven.

- ➢ Extroverts are the only ones who can pull it off.
- ➢ English is not my native tongue.

Skill No.65

Create a framework.

High achievement always takes place in the framework of high expectation. ~ Charles Kettering

Preparing for a presentation or making a speech may be challenging, particularly if we are starting from nothing. If you do not have a firm strategy, your entire presentation will look shaky and unconvincing.

The basic speech arrangement structure consists of five major components:

- ✓ Captivator of attention
- ✓ Introductory paragraph
- ✓ Body paragraph
- ✓ Concluding paragraph
- ✓ Call-to-activity

New frameworks are like climbing a mountain - the larger view encompasses rather than rejects the more restricted view. ~ Albert Einstein

Skill No.66

Make changes to your speech

Progress is impossible without change, and those who cannot change their minds cannot change anything.

~ George Bernard Shaw

After you have done the first draught, think about how you might improve your speech even more.

- ✓ Make your sentences easier to understand and shorter. - Start with the main action word when creating longer sentences.
- ✓ Important details and memorable events should be included.
- ✓ Incorporate strategically positioned intention sway stops.

The secret of change is to focus all of your energy not on fighting the old, but on building the new. ~ Socrates

Skill No.67

Taking a closer review of words

Review your goals twice every day in order to be focused on achieving them ~ Les Brown

Examining or reviewing a speech just takes a few seconds, and the best and ideal moment to do it is on the same day that you delivered it. Keep the speaker's delivery, as well as the speech's preparation, in mind.

A good, sympathetic review is always a wonderful surprise. ~ Joyce Carol

Would you say you were generally pleased with your recent speech? If not, why not? Have you achieved your goal? Is your key message reaching your intended audience? How sure are you that you will be able to deliver the presentation? Are you tenser throughout your speech than you were during your previous one?

Skill No.68

Assessment of audience feedback

"Remember to make sure your feedback is Kind, Helpful, specific accepting feedback leads to mastery."

Consider the input you received from the audience, such as your strengths and weaknesses.

Did you experiment with any new techniques during the planning stage or while delivering your speech? How do you get around a roadblock? How can anxiety, or any other cause not related to past discussions, be managed?

How long will your speech last? Is this a short or extended time span? Does it suggest that the presentation was given considerably faster than the speaker anticipated if the speaker concludes his speech far ahead of schedule? If the speaker has gone beyond to complete the speech, it is overflowing and speech reduction is required.

Skill No. 69

Know the 8 errors of Public Speaking and overcome

Thinking will not overcome fear but action will.
~W Clement stone.

Some speaking sins, similar to broken "ah" or "um", will not destine your presentation. With great substance, you can procure absolution from the audience for those wrongdoings.

Let us correct, the Seven Deadly Sins of Public Speaking

- Sloth: (Laziness) neglecting to get ready for speech / presentation.
- Envy: (Jealousy) accepting that incredible speakers are brought into the world with their abilities
- Lust: (Desire) controlling your nerves by envisioning the audience simple
- Gluttony: (Excess) accepting that excess words / content is in every case better
- Greed: speaking throughout your assigned time
- Wrath: (Anger) inflexibly responding to issues and losing your cool
- Pride: (Arrogance) putting yourself in front of the audience
- Comparison: (Contrast / Judgement) matching yourself with others and getting into stress.

Skill No. 70

Allow yourself some time.

It is so important to take time for yourself and find clarity. The most important relationship is the one you have with yourself. ~Diane von Furstenberg

Timing your speech every time you rehearse it will ensure you do not go over the five- to seven-minute time limit.

- ✓ You are not under any obligation to do properly.
- ✓ Your own style of inventiveness flourishes.
- ✓ Quiet time may be beneficial in addressing problems.
- ✓ Get a better understanding of whom you are.
- ✓ Getting more work done is necessary.
- ✓ Relax and be more welcoming of others around you.
- ✓ Investigate the possibilities of life.
- ✓ Spend time with those that matter to you.

Skill No. 71

Take it slowly & sturdily

I walk slowly, but i never walk backward
~ Abraham Lincoln

One of the most important things you can do to stay on track is to delegate not only the task but also the power.To boost your own productivity, slow down a little. Working for too long at a time may lead to mistakes, detours, and missed opportunities, among other things, all of which can lead to you working harder in the end.While a little jitter is necessary for many of us to maintain our competitive edge, too much unpredictability may backfire and hurt you.

If you are well rested rather than buzzing on adrenaline and caffeine, you will make better decisions, do better work, and recover faster.

It does not matter how slow you go, as long as you do not stop ~ Confucius

Skill No. 72

To prevent disappointment, arrive early.

Do not take rest after your first victory because if you fail in second, more lips are waiting to say that your first victory was luck.

Arriving early also helps you to show genuine excitement for the event. You will get the chance to meet and greet new individuals. It gives you plenty of time to be acquainted with the stage or presenting venue, as well as to practice using the microphone and any visual aids you will be using.

Before presenting a speech, it is usually a good idea to allow yourself plenty of time to relax. Extra time ensures you will not be late (even if Google Maps goes down) and allows you to get used to your presentation location.

Skill No. 73

Relax

"Sometimes the most productive thing you can do is relax".~ Mark Black

"Progressive Relaxation" helps in the reduction of muscle tension, allowing you to practice diaphragmatic breathing while remaining flexible and in control.

Long durations of being overly stressed might also lead to boredom. We should not only feel refreshed when we get up, but we should also feel refreshed throughout the day! Schedule in 5 minutes a few times during the day to relieve the tension and enhance your energy levels.

- ✓ Before taking the stage, take a deep breath and stretch.
- ✓ Before speaking, pause for a few seconds, smile, and count to three.
- ✓ It helps them to feel less stressed.
- ✓ Nervous Energy Can Be Transformed Into Enthusiasm

Skill No. 74

Keep your notes in check.

Check yourself before you wreck yourself ~ Meg Cabot

Maintain the order of your notes. If you must use notes, keep them to a minimum and do not read your speech aloud.

Skill No. 75

Make sure you learn from your mistakes.

When you make a mistake, there are only there things you should ever do about it: admit it, learn from it and do not repeat it. ~ Paul Bear Bryant

Everyone makes errors from time to time. The most essential thing is to remember what you have learned and keep going ahead. Mistakes can be useful in the future. We can truly learn from our mistakes and apply what we have learned to future situations. You will be able to quickly recall earlier mistakes and use them to solve problems more quickly.

Making errors really empowers us and strengthens us. You feel less exposed to error if you admit where you went wrong and own it. This improves our self-esteem and confidence, all of which are necessary for leadership responsibilities in the workplace.

Skill No. 76

Include Humour in speech

Good Humour is a tonic for mind and body. It is the best antidote for anxiety and depression. It is a business asset. It attracts and keeps friends. It lightens human burdens. It is the direct route to serenity and contentment. Grenville Kleiser

Even if you do not want to be a stand-up comedian, you may learn to deliver hilarious talks. Laughter raises the amount of oxygen in your blood, stimulates your heart, lungs,

and muscles, and boosts the amount of endorphins generated by your brain. Activate and deactivate the stress reaction in your body.

Humour, when used correctly, is a strong weapon that may help speakers in a variety of ways:

- ✓ The speaker and the listener form a relationship via humour.
- ✓ It energises and engages the audience.
- ✓ Humour may help people cope with their emotions.
- ✓ It aids in the retention of your points by the audience.

Skill No. 77

Self-concept

A person's self-concept is the core of his personality.
Joyce Brothers

Self-concept refers to how we see ourselves in terms of our actions, abilities, and distinguishing characteristics. Beliefs like "I am a nice friend" or "I am a compassionate person," The way we see ourselves has an impact on our motives, attitudes, and behaviors.

The Three Parts of Rogers' Self-Concept

- **Ideal self:** The person you desire to be is your ideal self. This individual possesses the characteristics or traits that you are striving toward or wishing to obtain. It is whom you imagine yourself to be if everything in your life went as planned.
- **Self-image:** Your self-image relates to how you view yourself right now. Physical attributes, psychological traits, and social positions all have an influence on your self-esteem.
- **Self-esteem:** How much you like, accept, and appreciate yourself all have a role in your self-concept, which is expressed as self-esteem. Self-esteem is influenced by a variety of variables, including how others see you and how you believe you compare to others.

Skill No. 78

Make use of common language.

A common language is a first step towards communication across cultural boundaries. Ethar Zuckerman

We are all quite busy. We do not want to waste time "translating" lengthy, complicated materials. Communicating in plain language saves time. We save money by saving time. It is good service and makes life simpler for the general people to use plain language.

People will grasp your content more quickly if you use simple language. Readers request explanations less often. Instead of using complicated terminology, impress your audience with your presentation and grasp of your topic.

For example, instead of "assist," say "help" or "use" instead of "utilise."

• Use simple language to get your message through in the smallest amount of time.

• There is a lower chance that your content will be misunderstood, so you will spend less time explaining it to others. Your readers are more likely to comprehend and follow directions if your text includes them.

Skill No. 79

Learn how to conclude a speech.

Many will Start Fast, few will Finish Strong
~ Gary Ryan Blair

The main piece of a speech is the end. Ensure you have a solid completion and a respectable start, and that they are close on schedule. Continuously reach a standstill before your crowd anticipates that you should realize there should be a superior method for closing your speech.

How might you end your speech as unquestionably as you opened it? Attempt these 12 hints:

1. The Title Close. Utilize the title of your speech as your end words.
2. The Circular Close. Allude back to your initial story or statement. Sum up the central matters in the work of art.
3. The Challenging Close. In the event that you were closing a speech on the significance of making a move,
4. The Invitation Close. In the event that you were closing a speech on the significance of engaging in the schooling system, you could say: Now is an ideal opportunity to do it and together we can. Make it happen!"

5. The Quotation Close. Observe a renowned citation and use it like a switch to lift the end of your speech.
6. The Repetitive Close. Observe an expression and design it in a dull configuration that strikes the rhythm of a drummer like a riddle, settle it. An objective, accomplish it."
7. The Singsong Close. Request that the crowd rehash an expression a couple of times in your speech as sing melody
8. The Suggestive Close. "Before I take questions, let me close with this point...."
9. The Benediction Close. "May God favour and keep you."
10. The Congratulatory Close. "I recognize every one of you and everybody in your association, and I anticipate your proceeded success."
11. The Proverbial Close. Track down a well-known expression and bend it to accommodate your message.
12. The Demonstration Close. Utilize a prop to flag the end of your speech.

Skill No. 80

Additional key features

Individual satisfaction and growth are improving. Individual happiness is one of the biggest benefits of learning how to deliver the best speech.

- It can help you overcome your anxiety of public speaking by increasing your vocabulary and fluency.
- Asserts your authority as a ruler.
- How do you set yourself out from the competition?
- Attracts the right clients/customers to your business
- Effectively delivers a tailored presentation
- Increases profit, sales, and operations of the firm.
- Improves verbal and nonverbal communication skills
- Improves critical thinking abilities
- It helps you grow and train people by improving innate communication, verbal and nonverbal abilities, and critical thinking skills.
- Develops leadership abilities and allows you to become a thinking leader.
- Boosts employee productivity and efficiency in the workplace.
- It allows you to have an impact on the world

Highly Effective Public Speaking Skills

- It gives you the ability to face your fears.
- Improved communication skills
- Increased authority skills
- Increased authority abilities
- Increased social influence
- Increased likelihood of meeting new people
- Anxiety and anxiousness while speaking in front of people are reduced.
- Improved memory
- Learn to discuss
- Improved memory
- Increased influence ability
- Have excellent listening skills.

Thank you

Y. Narasimha Raja

9 798887 177502

Printed by Libri Plureos GmbH in Hamburg, Germany